THE POLITICS OF
BLACK
WOMEN'S HAIR

also by the author

Being Black
Ladies of the Night
Loving This Man

THE POLITICS OF BLACK WOMEN'S HAIR

ALTHEA PRINCE

INSOMNIAC PRESS

Library and Archives Canada Cataloguing in Publication

Prince, Althea, 1945-
      The politics of black women's hair / Althea Prince.

ISBN 978-1-897178-87-4

      1. Women, Black--Health and hygiene.
2. Women, Black--Social conditions. 3. Hair--Social
aspects. 4. Hairdressing--Social aspects. I. Title.

HQ1161.P75 2009   305.48'896   C2009-904624-5

The publisher gratefully acknowledges the support of the Canada Council, the Ontario Arts Council and the Department of Canadian Heritage through the Book Publishing Industry Development Program.

Printed and bound in Canada

Insomniac Press,
520 Princess Avenue
London, Ontario, Canada, N6B 2B8
www.insomniacpress.com

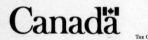

THE CANADA COUNCIL | LE CONSEIL DES ARTS
FOR THE ARTS | DU CANADA
SINCE 1957 | DEPUIS 1957

ONTARIO ARTS COUNCIL
CONSEIL DES ARTS DE L'ONTARIO

Dedication

With love to my lifelong friends, Juanita Nanton,
and Holly Peters...
Thank you for all of the love,
from pitter-patter feet through womanhood.

Acknowledgements

What more can a writer ask for, if not a caring publisher – Mike O'Connor, and a good editor – Gillian Rodgerson. Thank you both. I also thank Managing Editor, Dan Varrette for his kind help as we went into the finish line.

Friends and family come next: Thank you all for continuing to be right in the pocket with loving support.

There are a few other people to add to the mix: the mothers of Black girls who agreed to speak with me about their relationship with their daughters' hair. They are Veronica Ciandre, Skira Martinez, Elaine Nash, Andrea Oliver, Glenda Prince, and Itah Sadu. I also thank the daughters of Elaine Nash (Nina and Rayna) for granting me interviews. Thank you to Taija Ryan, and Maxine Greene in Toronto for sharing your views on Black women and hair. I also thank a third young woman in Toronto who asked to remain anonymous, and whose comments about hair are included.

I am deeply grateful to Dr. Janis Prince Inniss for her essay about her hair-journey.

Lastly, I thank my daughter, Mansa Trotman for allowing me to include her signature poem about Black women's hair.

Contents

Beginning the Walk

...journeying from the core...

I have come to accept that a Black woman has a personal relationship with her hair—it can be either a good relationship or a bad relationship. I have yet to see anything in-between. During plantation slavery in the Americas, some light-skinned women who had African blood in them would shave all of the hair off their heads. In this way, they hoped to be able to pass for white and escape the slave catcher.

Clearly, the texture of hair that people of African descent possess is something that attracted attention very early in both the "Old World" and the "New World," and this historical trajectory of hair, beauty, and acceptability continues to determine Black women's interpretation of themselves in society. People of African descent appeared in nineteenth-century literature mostly through the use of negative images, especially those of their hair. One famous example is that of a little girl named "Topsy," a character in Harriet Beecher Stowe's book *Uncle Tom's Cabin*. Topsy is described with particular attention paid to the details of her "woolly" hair.

Beecher Stowe's novel is set during the era of plantation slavery in the U.S.A. The author describes Topsy's hair as "woolly" and braided in small plaits that stuck out "in every direction" all over her head. American artists have faithfully reproduced this image since the book was first published in 1852. It was hailed as a humane story showing the cruelty of slavery, and is considered one of the influences that led to the American Civil War. The Anti-Slavery Movement embraced the book, although African Americans in modern times have decried many of its paternalistic assumptions about the relationships between slave and master. They have also objected to the simple-mindedness that the author attributes to the Black characters, in particular, to Topsy and Uncle Tom.

While modern scholars—mostly ones of African descent—have vilified Beecher Stowe for her descriptions of the Black characters in her novel, she was not alone. In 1895, Florence Kate Upton, an American living in England, created a character named "Golliwogg" in the children's book *The Adventures of Two Dutch Dolls and a Golliwogg*. He was described as "a horrid sight, the blackest gnome." Moreover, it was commonly known that Upton took the physical characteristics of the character from a "Blackface" minstrel[1] doll that she had had as a child in the U.S.A. Golliwogg's description was not unlike that of Topsy: he had shoe-polish-black skin; large red lips; and thick, unkempt, woolly hair.

In Upton's story, Golliwogg is noted for his kindness—a personality trait attributed to the "Blackface" minstrels whom he resembled. Golliwogg became a very popular doll that every self-respecting white child in Europe, and a large number in the U.S.A., possessed. It is important to note, however, that when Golliwogg became "*the* golliwog" and was turned into a doll, his character could be quite menacing. He also turned up in Enid Blyton's children's books, where he is sometimes portrayed as kindly, but more often than not, he is a sinister character. All of the Enid Blyton books that I read as a child contained a not-so-nice golliwog. I recall that I wondered where the author had got the idea for such a creature. Given that he did not look like anything I had ever seen before, I never equated him with anyone in my country, community, or life. I thought he was entirely fictional, created in the author's wild imagination—out of thin air, so to speak. Of course, my Caribbean childhood did not include any references to minstrel shows, and I had never seen a golliwog doll.

Golliwog iconography remains in Europe today, although it is hardly seen in North America any more; and children of African descent in Europe still suffer the humiliation of occasionally being called "wog," an insulting derivative of "golliwog." The term "wog"—used during the British colonial days in the Middle East, India, the Mediterranean, and North Africa—was applied in modern times in the U.K. to Black people from the Caribbean, Africa, to people from India, and to virtually anyone who is dark-skinned. White children equated Black children's hair with the woolly head of the golliwog, and recently, Black parents have had the book removed from the formal educational system in the U.K.

The removal of the book has not stopped the golliwog from appearing in the racist consciousness of some people, however. In England, in late 2008 and early 2009, the golliwog caused quite a stir by being on the lips of first a parliamentarian, and then journalist Carol Thatcher, and finally showing up in doll form in the Queen's own Buckingham Palace souvenir shop. It appears that while it is possible to remove the offensive golliwog from libraries, bookstores, and shops, the character appears to have so taken hold of some people's consciousness that they are loathe to relinquish it. First the parliamentarian, and then the journalist, argued that the golliwog reference was "just a joke," and had to be pressed into apologizing for connecting him with Black people.

I sometimes think that somewhere in the world, forever and a day, there will be a group of Black people who come upon a golliwog book in a school library that has to be removed before it attacks their children's consciousness. There are a few of those kinds of books still "out there." I recall that in Toronto in the 1960s, it took strong community lobbying to get Little Black Sambo [2]. books removed from the school libraries. In this series of books intended for children, the character "Little Black Sambo" is a close facsimile of the golliwog with the same wild hair, exaggeratedly black skin, and big, bright-red lips.

Hair is entirely public. People can hide it on occasion, but it is always there—a symbol that is open to interpretation by others about who they deem us to be. For Black women, hair clearly represents something about which they have, or have had issues, experiences, and journeys. This appears to be so, no matter the texture or length of a Black woman's hair. I think it is so whether Black women wear their hair long or short, natural or straightened, and whether they wear it in dreadlocks or braided—with or without extensions. The hair on a Black woman's head is treated as if it is a separate entity from the rest of her body—she and her family treat it that way, and other Black people treat it that way. In the wider community, the Black woman's natural hair falls low on the scale of beauty. This is no surprise, as it is clear that the dominant beauty paradigm that gets affirmed falls within the Eurocentric, hegemonic culture. This beauty paradigm promotes an ideal of European facial features, light or white skin, and straight hair.

Fortunately, I have seen many more good relationships with hair than I've seen bad ones among Black women. Beginning this book, I did not fool myself into thinking that my own positive vision of things was the general state of being. On the contrary, there are daily reminders of the bad relationships that some Black women have with their hair. One of the questions I wanted to address in this collection of essays is: How bad are these relationships? There seemed to be a wide range of experiences, and even more interesting, a variety of responses to these experiences. My conversations with women confirmed that not everyone emerges battered, bruised, and insecure about her hair. Some women have transcended the psychological, social, and cultural attacks on their hair, and are, in fact, useful voices for other Black women to hear.

This book brings some of those voices together for that purpose, yes, and also to present a bird's-eye view of things. Many people come into contact with the Black woman and the hair phenomenon, and it has seeped into mainstream popular culture in some new and disturbing forms. For some, there is merely curiosity. This book is not written to satisfy that curiosity, but rather, for those people who are genuinely seeking understanding about Black women's relationships with their hair. Most importantly, it will be useful to Black women. And...perhaps this is a book that someone like Barbara Walters could use to satisfy her curiosity, rather than pulling at her Black women guests' hair and asking if they're wearing wigs, as she's done on-air on at least two occasions. It might also let her understand the culpability of the Eurocentric, hegemonic yardstick that is at the core of Black women's journey with hair, and her own attitude to Black women's hair.

Hair is at the heart of many Black women's sense of who they are in the wider world that they navigate daily. At one time, concern about hair included their positioning themselves on society's yardstick of beauty, and sometimes it was focused on racial identity. More recently, however, hairstyles have come to be signifiers within the Black community, and in the wider community, with rendered meanings that may or may not be correct. In some instances, women who wear their hair in its natural form are assumed to be radical, or at least progressive, and maybe lesbian. On the other hand, women with straightened hair are often assumed to be conservative.

Misreading a person's hair as a signifier can have repercussions that could be trivial in a social situation but far-reaching in the worst-case scenario. For many Black women, hair is just hair, and the choices they make are connected to convenience and ease— not to their politics or sexual preference. Nonetheless, they can still be judged with a social or political interpretation of who they are, based solely on their hairstyle.

Clearly, Black women do not all think alike, nor do they make choices for the same reasons. There may be a large divergence in the significance of a particular hairstyle among Black women. For example, the Afro was a signifier of radical Black cultural nationalism in the 1960s and 70s. This is no longer necessarily the meaning that is attached to it by the women who wear it. The interpretation persists, however, especially by people who lived through that radical era.

When I decided to write a book about Black women's social and political issues surrounding hair, my first inclination was to keep the content light and deliver a message that would be useful to mothers of Black girls, to young Black women, and to the public at large. The message, I felt, needed to be about making a simple truth self-evident: that Black girls come out of the womb with beautiful hair. I consider that to be a pure and simple truth and wanted to write some words that would enable the dissemination of this truth so that it filled every nook and cranny—or at least those I could reach. And lest I stand accused of preaching, let me say that it is not missionary zeal that motivates me; rather, it is another simple truth that spurred me to this action: I continue to meet Black women and Black girls who have had traumatic experiences with their hair, or who have their hair caught up in social and political issues. To their credit, these women and girls are seeking to know, to understand, and to embrace a new vision of hair and their connections with it. So we journey on, seeking to know the truth about our hair...communicate it to the hearts of Black girls...so that they will reclaim it in their lives...and bodies...for hair is just another part of the body.

How would I chart the journey through these two pure and simple truths? I opened my mind, heart, and spirit to allowing them to arrive on whatever ripples of energy they chose. It would not be a direct route that I would take through the journey...I wanted there to be movements in harmony with others along the route...not just a litany of my personal experiences. I also dispensed with the idea of collecting data from a large number of respondents. There were other books that did that. What did I want? Something personal. Conversations. Words that make heart-connections between the reader and the things discussed in the book.

I decided on the personal essay. I felt sure that that form was what would work for this kind of personal life project. I was conducting a humanistic seek-and-go-find...I expected that a few branches would swirl with logic, and with humour...that would be just wonderful! I would not spend much time on extreme political "reasonings"...I knew that I would sidestep judgements, such as: if you straighten your hair, or even take some of the curls out of it with a flat-iron, then you are not a real Black woman. Those rules were the rules of the 1960s and 70s, and while they served the time, this is indeed a different time and clime. Today, I do not think that radical Black politics—the political platform of Black cultural nationalism—is a site of consciousness for the majority of Black women. And I think that for those women for whom it *is* a site of consciousness, there are no longer the rules that deny access to Black women with straightened hair.

All of this is included in the discussions in this collection. I have been sure to maintain my objective to bring something to the healing of the damage done to the souls of Black girls and women through their hair. For the hegemonic control of the standards of beauty surrounding Black women's hair has done so much damage that I do not want to add to it by attacking or condemning any woman for her choice of hairstyle. Yet, I discuss Black women's hair honestly, raising issues about which they are already talking—and indeed, have always talked—within the contexts raised in the essays in the collection. My focus is on the links between Black women's hair and psychological empowerment in the lives of Black girls and women. I decided that when the details of hair grooming were included, it would be neither to condemn nor praise; rather, it would be to enhance the more important discussion of building emotional strength.

This is the kind of book that I needed to read when I was a

young girl, begging my mother to allow me to "iron" my hair. [3] All of the friends who mattered to me had their hair ironed; my older sisters also had theirs ironed, and I felt that I was missing out on something. It was my turn for this rite of passage. How I yearned for the bangs that they all sported! Perhaps nothing I read would have stopped that yearning...it was so strong...it was so important to fit in...to be a part of the group—especially in terms of looks. The yearning of a teenager to fit in is a very powerful motivational force—I did not rest until I got permission to iron my hair.

I want this book to consider what might resolve that kind of consciousness for young, Black girls when dealing with their hair. What could replace or circumvent the yearning to fit in with the group? Will it take another group consciousness? How do Black girls grow into Black women who are secure enough not to be "taken down" by their hair? The book's focus includes the joy of hair, the normalcy of hair, and the ease that it is possible to have concerning hair. For some women, it is an epiphany that has brought them to such a place of seeing, of living, of b-e-i-n-g; and they speak about it openly.

I believe that some discussion of the impact of the media on the beauty yardstick is warranted, and it's included to enhance and locate the discussion. I have, however, determinedly avoided vitriolic haranguing of mainstream cultural hegemony—and especially the media—for its treatment and placement of Black women on the beauty yardstick. That is perhaps due, but it is not the project that I am *feeling* at this time. I am *feeling* a project that resonates with me as stridently as Toni Morrison's little, yet large, book *The Bluest Eye*.

The novel hit me right in the gut with a ferocious expunging of the violence of a hegemonic control that defines standards of beauty in one particular way. The main character, Pecola, is an eleven-year-old Black girl who believes that she is ugly because of the way she is treated by the people in her life. She notices that everyone in her world uses symbols of "whiteness" as the epitome of beauty, and so she wishes for beautiful, blue eyes. She believes that if she could have blue eyes then people would notice that she exists; and so every night, Pecola prays for blue eyes. Finally, she becomes insane, thus escaping the world in which it is impossible for her to be beautiful.

What resonates with me about Pecola is not her descent into madness but the veracity that the beauty yardstick holds for her. Its grip is so all-pervasive—so powerful—that she believes it completely. She catapults into a vain attempt to actually *become* white, believing in the possibility of becoming beautiful.

Pecola's truth is the hegemonic, viselike grip of society's yardstick of beauty. This yardstick penetrates consciousness, and is internalized by the individual to become their truth. It is that yardstick that Black women use to determine the value of their hair. Unlike Pecola—and because of Pecola—I know that beauty cannot be set up on a single yardstick—that all people are not the same—and that all hair is not the same. I know that everyone came into the world beautiful, just as they are. This much I know. And that is what I wanted to be the focus of this book.

Morrison's staggering presentation of hegemonic control hit some deep, bass chords in my gut. At the time when I read it, I walked around looking into the eyes of Black girls, trying to see the extent to which they accepted this Pecola-truth. "Do they wish they had blue eyes?" And for a while, through fake contact lenses, some brown-eyed Black women *did* acquire blue, green, and hazel eyes! Thankfully, that fad did not last long...but for a time, a few Black women in the entertainment industry looked as if they were possessed—like Chucky, the demonic doll that comes to life in the movie of the same name. Their blue, green, and hazel eyes, sitting incongruously in their dark faces, would look eerily out from magazines and television screens.

For a while, I wrote some brainstorming notes about my own experiences with hair—the memories that shape my sense of what is beautiful hair. I wanted to speak from the heart about my assault on my hair with an iron-comb. I would connect up the dots between this assault and the belief, like Pecola, in what makes beautiful hair.

As I began to write in earnest, I felt overwhelmed by how much there was that I *did indeed* find myself saying—not just about hair but also about the whole area of the hegemonic control of standards of beauty. My thoughts also spilled over into style, language, and a whole number of related topics; and those areas also climbed into my project...or at least into my thinking. I was soon reluctantly immersed in an expanded rehashing of the overall hegemonic standards of beauty—skin colour and other anatomical features.

My reluctance came from a feeling of déjà vu, a feeling of being there, over and over again. Having heard it, read it, listened to it, lived it in the 60s and 70s, I had no desire to simply go back over the very same issues in the same rhetorical voice.

I found that there were a small number of books on the topic of the politics of Black women's hair in the U.S.A., and none in Canada, the Caribbean, or the U.K. There are also two films—both of which I saw some time ago—and there are a number of websites (most of them originating in the U.S.A.) where Black women discuss the cultural and political issues surrounding hair.

There are only three from Canada, and two from the U.K.

The research began to arc out, almost as if it had a life of its own; it branched out—not just geographically but also topically. I knew that hair was important...and yet...there was much more material about the many other modern-day manifestations of the entrenchment of white hegemonic culture and its impact on Black women's sense of beauty. I toyed with the idea of writing about skin colour, facial features, lips, buttocks, hips—indeed, all aspects of the Black woman's anatomy. I also thought about including films, television, comic books, and magazines. On and on I went—foraging my way through images and words in popular culture. It soon became clear that there was simply too much to write about...I could not cram it all into one book. And even if I did pull it all together under one banner, it would no longer be the little book I wanted to write. I could see the project *morphing* into a sociological rendering with sections entitled "Aesthetics, Race, Class, and Gender" and "Black Aesthetics: Nurture versus Nature." There would definitely also have to be a section entitled "The Impact of Cultural Hegemony on Black Women's Sense of Self."

So...I returned to hair. Pecola was still with me, guiding me to see hair the way she saw blue eyes. Pecola was my key. Some modern-day naked truths leapt screaming into my consciousness. The first incident, which I will discuss in more depth in the essay "Versions of Hair," happened in 1998 when a Black woman in the U.S.A. was denied membership in a sorority because she wore her hair in dreadlocks. I was struck by the depth of the feelings about hair! Years later, when I began this collection of essays, the experience of that young woman would return to haunt me. I decided to include experiences of people outside of my own particular, as this would bring breadth to the book.

I invited ten women to contribute to the discussion by allowing me to interview them about hair. Dr. Janis Prince Inniss, who is a sociologist and family therapist, contributed a "guest essay" that, tinged with wry humour, traces her journey with hair from childhood through adulthood. The women whose voices are included in the book are from Canada, South America (Guyana), the Caribbean, the U.S.A., and the U.K. These women's perspectives have enhanced the collection, adding not only to the expansion of the discussion but also bringing an international aspect to it.

Six of the women are mothers, and speak about experiences with their own and their daughters' hair. They are: Veronica Ciandre, Skira Martinez, Elaine Nash, Andrea Oliver, Glenda Prince, and Itah Sadu.

Two of the interviewees are young (30s) African American women: Nina and Raina Nash; and three interviewees are young (20s and 30s) African Canadian women: Taija Ryan, Maxine Greene, and a third woman who wishes to remain anonymous.

African Canadian poet Mansa Trotman's signature poem on Black women's hair is at the end of the book.

Madam C. J. Walker (born Sarah Breedlove in Louisiana), while living in Denver, Colorado in 1905, popularized the use of a metal comb ("iron-comb") that when heated, transformed Black women's hair from tight curls into smooth, straight hair. She became a millionaire from the iron-comb, and from the hair pomades that were used with it. She also developed a line of hair pomades that promoted hair growth. Many Black people criticized Madame Walker for creating products that made Black women's hair imitate white women's long, straight hair. Although she did not invent the hot iron-comb, she was the one who popularized its use. Church ministers, therefore, led the attack against her, accusing her of going against God's natural design.

In 1970, the late Beverly Mascoll, an African Canadian woman from Nova Scotia, living in Toronto, began selling hair-care and other beauty-care products for Black women. I have heard her speak about the early days of building her company, using the trunk of her car, and having her baby with her on her rounds. Out of frustration at not finding products for Black women in Canada, she approached the owner of the African American company Johnson Products to be their agent in Canada. Mascoll went on to build a multimillion-dollar company, supplying and distributing products for the care of Black women's hair and skin. The Black population in Toronto was a relatively new one, at least, in large numbers. By 1970, when Mascoll began her own company, large groups of African peoples were arriving in Toronto from the Caribbean, Africa, and England.

NOTES

1. "Blackface" is a style of theatrical makeup used by white men who performed "minstrel shows" by imitating Black musical and dance forms. Beginning in the 1830s, they created a savage parody of Black Americans that lasted for more than a hundred years. They used burnt cork and later greasepaint or shoe polish to blacken their skin and exaggerate their lips; woolly wigs, white gloves, tailcoats, or ragged clothes completed the transformation into caricatures of Black people. Later, Black artists also performed in Blackface. The minstrel-show era contributed to the racist images of Black people in plantation slavery as dancing, smiling buffoons.

2. *The Story of Little Black Sambo* is a children's book written by Scottish author Helen Bannerman. First published in London in 1899, the book is clearly set in India where Bannerman lived at the time. Little Black Sambo is intended to be Indian, but the illustrations in the original European version portray him using Black minstrel iconography, with black skin, wild hair, and bright-red lips. The book has been widely criticized by Black people in the twentieth century throughout the world.

3. Hair is "ironed" using a hot metal comb such as the one made popular by Madame C. J. Walker.

Rituals

...touch a black woman's hair...

In an introduction that I wrote to Trey Anthony's play *Da Kink in My Hair*, I noted that she suggests that there is a spiritual connection that happens for Black women when you touch their hair—that is, when you are grooming their hair. One of Anthony's characters says: "If you want to know about a Black woman, touch her hair." That suggestion resonates strongly with me, for I have always thought of Black women's hair-grooming as a ritual—a spiritual happening that loosens Black women's emotions and their tongues.

I was struck by the resonance with the same sentiment in my novel, *Loving This Man*. The main character and her mother look forward to their hair-combing and plaiting (braiding) sessions. The mother combs and plaits the daughter's hair, and as the daughter becomes a teenager, she enjoys combing and plaiting her mother's hair. During these sessions, they share intimate feelings with each other—things that do not move easily from heart, to throat, to tongue.

African women in the Caribbean did not invent this hair-grooming ritual. In the traditional West African societies of our ancestors, hair-grooming (and by extension, hair-braiding) is an ancient art handed down from generation to generation of women. Girls usually have their hair groomed by their mothers, or an older relative: a sister, an aunt, or an extended family member.

These hair-grooming sessions among women in traditional West African societies have always been presented as creating a bond between mothers and their daughters...or girls and women. I note that cooking is also usually presented in the same way. These rituals are used to pass on life lessons and any other instruction that would sometimes come in the form of stories. The stories could be about family members, or people in the community, or mythical characters: human, and/or animal, as is the case with Anansi stories in the Caribbean[1].

I drew on my own hair-combing sessions with my daughter to create the scene between the mother and the daughter in *Loving This Man*. I consciously created these experiences with my daughter. I had wished for my own hair-combing sessions, with my mother and my older sisters, to continue for longer than they did. My mother never had the time to engage in such luxuries as creating alone-time with each of her girl children. She had twelve children—five of whom were girls. She was a seamstress, and took in work from people in the neighbourhood. She also made all of our clothes, including my brothers' shirts. In addition, for several years during my childhood, she ran a small grocery store that was attached to our home.

I was the youngest of my mother's five daughters, and so our hair—mine, and that of my sister who was four years older than me—was washed, combed, and plaited by our three older sisters. By the time I was eleven years old, the three oldest sisters had gone to England, and it became very clear to me that combing my hair represented an unpleasant additional task for my already over-burdened mother. How did I know? Well, she would tap me on the head with the back of the comb if I did not sit still, and throughout our hair-combing sessions, she would complain about having to comb my hair and my sister's hair.

Before this time, my mother's combing and plaiting my hair was so rare that I craved it with every fibre of my being. It repre-sented for me a time to have her all to myself, to have closeness with her—but Mama had no time to sit with my head in her lap while she combed my hair. In fact, she soon resorted to arranging to pay a young woman in the neighbourhood a shilling to comb our hair.

This young woman was a neighbour's daughter, and on the first day that I was sent to her, I actually looked forward to going. I set off bright and early in the morning, clutching a shilling, a comb, and a jar of Vaseline. I was an inquisitive child who loved to know the details of people's lives. I especially liked to see the inside of their homes, and it was the first time that I would get to see the inside of our neighbours' home...at least, that's what I ex-pected. On the contrary, my hair was combed on the gallery of the house, and I barely got a fleeting glimpse of the drawing room (living room) when my hair-comber opened the door in answer to my timid knock.

She came out onto the gallery, and without a word sat me down on a chair, stood behind me, and proceeded to pull and tug my hair into submission. It was vicious...it was tight...it was painful...and it was pretty to look at when it was done. The process was so painful that I completely forgot about thinking any interesting thoughts while it was happening. That was something I was accustomed to doing while my hair was being plaited by my sisters or my mother. From the time my hair-comber put her hands on my head, the only thought I had was: Please, God, make her stop!

I had even hoped to have a conversation with my hair-comber because I had never had an opportunity to do so before that morning. She was a good bit older than I was, and had been out of school for some time. We attended different schools, and there was no time together on the street because all of the children in my family were forbidden to play outside of our gate. However, to my disappointment, there was to be no conversation...none! That young woman never even spoke two words to me; she performed the task she was assigned in complete silence. When she needed my head to be turned this way or that, she simply moved it into place by using one hand like a vise around my forehead. Her grip was so deep that her fingers left a hot, throbbing spot at each temple. Just as it wore off, she would grip my forehead again, turning my head sharply, this way or that. At least she didn't tap my head with the back of the comb as my mother had done; although that was a small mercy for which I do not recall being particularly grateful.

Realistically, I could not have engaged in conversation with my hair-comber. All of my attention and nerves were focused on stifling my screams before they could leave my mouth. My head was put through the most severe pain and torture it, and I, had ever experienced. In a flash of the comb, my thick hair was pulled into tight rows of Congo, as cornrows were called in Antigua. The hair on my head seemed to grow in the hands of my hair-comber because when she was finished, my plaits looked much longer than they had ever done. She so determinedly pulled my hair as she moved it into three-strand-continuous rows of Congo that it became straighter, thus giving it more length. I am quite sure that she was not focused on lengthening my plaits; it was just the way she worked on hair.

My eyes were watering as I handed my hair-comber the shilling that my mother had given me to pay her. She cleaned the comb of the tufts of hair that she had pulled from my head and pressed them into my palm; and I remembered that I had always heard that you should burn your hair, rather than throwing it in the rubbish bin. This was because, my mother told me, that it was possible to use people's hair to work *obeah*[2]. on them. Even in the midst of my pain, I wondered if my hair-comber was thinking about that *obeah* story. At that moment, I did not care about my tufts of hair; I could not imagine that *obeah* would be any worse than the experience I had just endured. Gingerly, I walked down the steps of the gallery without looking down for fear that it would hurt even more if I moved my head in any way. The pain worked its way all the way down my body, and seemed to settle in my navel. My eyes felt as if they had been stretched out of their sockets and moved to a different location in my face—they felt closer to my ears somehow.

When I got to our gate and reached up to undo the latch, I felt a corresponding ripple of pain all around the edges of my head. It seemed that any little movement above the neck also activated severe pain in the roots of my hair. A few minutes later, I discovered that when I spoke, the skin around my temples hurt severely. Soon, I realised that if I turned my head to the left or to the right, the back of my neck felt as if it would explode. Smiling brought tears; laughing brought screams.

I looked in the bathroom mirror and tugged at the plaits to

no avail; it was as if they were nailed to my head. I would have to manage somehow, but what was I to do? I discovered that standing still was the best position of all, especially if at the same time I did not move a single muscle in my face. If I needed to look around, I turned my entire body. Somehow, I got through the day, dizzily making my way through classes, games (sports), and conversation. There was never a moment that I was not aware of the pain in my head, my hair, my neck, and my life!

Sleep came fitfully that night. Every touch of my head to the pillow brought me pain. I finally found a way to sleep with my face turned sideways into the pillow so that it did not touch my head. The next morning, I woke up with a stiff neck—a firm crook in my neck that made the next hair-combing session even more nightmarish.

In those days, there was no leaving your plaits in place for weeks, or even days at a time, as is the case today. Respectability demanded that ones hair had to be combed and plaited every single day; so the next morning, and every morning thereafter, off I went for another session with my hair-comber. Her attack on my head did not get any easier to tolerate, and she remained silent as she exacted this daily torture. Sometimes, I would leave the gallery with tears in my eyes that did not come from any sadness in my heart; they were simply my body's response to the pulling at my temples and the tautness of the plaits.

At first, it never occurred to me to complain to my mother, or to anyone...in those days children did what they were told. By day three or four, however, I developed a rash around my face and at the back of my head that looked like razor bumps. I finally complained to my mother, and she shrugged it off, saying that it was just from the hair being pulled tight. She tugged at each strand with her fingers, and it helped to loosen the plaits so that I could breathe more easily. I fully expected her to speak with my hair-comber about it but nothing was said. The next day, off I went as usual, comb, Vaseline, and shilling in hand, to receive my day's torture. This time, I had figured out how to loosen the plaits in the way that my mother had done; and from then on, I had a barely manageable level of pain. In my adult life, I have discovered from doctors that I actually have a very high pain threshold. This information put my hair-comber's torture into even more stark reality because it means that for the average person, the pain would have been even greater.

As I look back, I wonder at the power of the silencing that prevented me from complaining loudly about the daily assault on my head. I was not the only one who endured it; my older sister had the same experience but I do not recall her complaining either. In school, many girls had the same tight, straining rows of Congo, and yet, we did not even complain to each other about the pain we endured to get them!

After a week or so, I found my voice; little girl though I was, I broke the silence expected from an eleven year old. I asked my hair-comber to make the plaits slacker. She seemed displeased but I didn't care; I was tired of the pain, and since no one else was going to rescue me, I figured I would put a stop to it myself.

The pulling continued unabated but at least the plaits were done less tightly...most of the time. I never did find sufficient power of voice to speak to her about the pulling. I had to stay on the alert about the plaiting because she would suddenly slip back to creating mind-altering, tight-tight plaits. Soon, I stopped getting the rash around the edges of my hair. Meanwhile, my hair-comber and I settled into a weird kind of friendly communication. I started saying a few words of greeting to her, asking her how she was, and she would respond with a little smile and a murmur. This lasted for two years.

I couldn't wait to be old enough to look after my own hair. By the time I was thirteen, through sheer strength of will, and much practising on my own head, I figured out how to plait Congo. Now that I look back at how I managed to learn just by experimentation, I realize that for two years, my focus had been on what my hair-comber's fingers were doing in my head. It is as if she imprinted the method through my scalp...like a drumbeat. When I worked on my hair, moving it into rows of Congo, it was the memory of her fingers in my hair that I emulated...without the pain, of course! My mother and my sister did not plait Congo, and so my hair-comber was my only model. I became really good at it—so much so, that my mother agreed that I could look after my own hair. This meant that besides saving her a whole shilling every day, I was happy that I no longer had to endure the daily morning torture. No longer would I have to keep an eye on the tightness of the plaits, constantly beseeching my hair-comber to "please make them slacker."

After my experience with the hair-comber, I promised myself that if I had a daughter, I would never let her suffer any pulling of her hair. When she was a baby, I groomed her hair so gently that she would fall asleep; and I would continue to work on her hair, using my fingers to smooth it into twists. I sought the right kinds of soft brushes, "tearless" shampoos, and hairdressings that promised to smooth out knots. As she grew older, I made our hair-combing sessions into playful times when we talked about things that made her laugh, or made her eyes open wide in wonder. Sometimes, like the daughter in my novel, she simply put her head in my lap and went to sleep. I felt happy. I had broken the cycle of causing a Black girl to feel pain because of her hair. No matter what choices she makes about her hair, they will come from a place outside of childhood physical pain, or a belief that her hair was "a problem."

Interestingly, hair is the focus of one of my daughter's first published poems, "Look What the Future Hath Wrought," found at the end of this book. In it, she takes a gentle, laughing look at how Black women have allowed hair to control their well-being, internalizing the belief that to be feminine, they have to have straight hair.

...can't look like a duplicate of him
gotta look like a woman with
hair that swings when you walk
hair that moves when you laugh
hair that he can run his hands through and not get stuck...

I am pleased that she came to those conclusions without any overt coaching from me. At the same time, I feel certain that my treatment and behaviour surrounding hair must have affected her political "take" on Black women's hair. I hope I have passed on a healthy baton.

NOTES

1. Anansi stories originated in Ghana, West Africa, among Akan-speaking peoples. They feature a trickster spider character named Anansi. The stories are told somewhat differently in the Caribbean, although they still contain Anansi's general characteristics.

2. *Obeah* is a retention from the Orisha religion of Yoruba people in Nigeria, West Africa. It is now considered a magical or mystical practice.

Who I Am Is in My Hair

by Dr. Janis Prince Inniss

Who I am is in my hair. I am not my hair (I agree with singer/songwriter India.Arie) but who I am is reflected in my hair, in the way I wear it.

I remember living in Amelia's Ward, Guyana, and having my hair washed at the sink by the back door every other Sunday. I must have been about eight years old when we lived there. I guess we had a laundry set-up at the back door—sink and faucet—which would have been unusual at that time in that place. Anyway, Mummy would commence to wash my hair, and with my head bent over in the sink, I would pray not to drown. I certainly had a fear of drowning, which was in no way diminished by these experiences. I would be terrified that I would get soap in my eyes—which seemed to happen most weeks—and that there would be so much water in my face that I would feel like I was drowning. Boy, that soap would burn! It made me feel crazed, like

I wanted to hop around screaming in the sandy yard, but we would press on with Mummy trying to cajole all of my hair into being washed at the same time. Not soon enough, the washing would be over, but there was no relief in that, as the scene of the crime would move to our living room. Mummy would put me to sit between her knees and she would struggle to comb out my dripping hair. Eventually, that task done, she would "slack plait" my hair—making about eight loose braids to allow my hair to dry. I would go back to life before the washing began, and every now and then after some hours had passed, Mummy would begin scratching around in my plaits to check on the status of my hair. Satisfied that my hair was bone dry (crunch, crunch), the ritual would continue with me returning to my spot on the living room floor. This time around, Mummy would "grease my scalp" rather meticulously and then comb my hair for school the next day. I hated all of this! All of it! Mummy got so exasperated, seemed so beaten by my hair at each stage of the experience; it was as if my hair was to be conquered and she couldn't.

We were still living in the same house, when, at about age ten, I spent one very frustrating Saturday morning in my bedroom, trying to make a ponytail. I remember that bedroom in the back of the house and how I struggled with my hair in it. That Saturday I cried and cried with frustration, as I could not make my hair do what I wanted. I just could not get *all* of it into my holder. Eventually, I did, although it was not a neat job. That was a turning point for me; I would not be beat by my own hair, but I was never satisfied with the way Mummy combed it. To be fair, after struggling with the washing, I think she felt she had earned the right to coast with its styling. She did not seem to feel any more mastery over combing my hair than washing it, and seemed to be more concerned that she had done her job by sending me off each day looking neat, than with coming up with new and exciting hairstyles. This meant that most days my hairstyle was what she called "two fat plaits." Usually, she added wide ribbons the colour of my outfit at the base of each pigtail. For variety, sometimes she would place the ribbons at the *ends* of each braid! I found this rather boring, so I would occasionally complain, and in honour of my request for a new style, Mummy would comb my hair in two— with the part from ear to ear! She seemed to find this fairly amusing, but I did not. By age ten, I realized that I would have to fend for myself if I wanted hairstyle variety.

So I took over the hair combing, while Mummy did the washing. The pain of washing never improved, but at least I could look the way I wanted. And this was good because from the age of thirteen, I spent increasing amounts of time away from Mummy, and needed to be able to take care of myself—or at least of my appearance. Initially, I think she continued to do the washing, but then when I moved *countries*, I had to make some new plans: I went to the hairdresser for a while but that was pretty expensive, so I learned how to wash and set my own hair. By then my hair was permed...I think that started when I lived in Toronto. I began to limit my forays to the beauty parlour to having my hair trimmed and permed every—how often are you supposed to perm your hair? I've forgotten. Also, in that era, my brother dated a hairdresser who loved doing my hair: a win-win situation, as she scored points with my brother, and I got free hair maintenance and tips.

When I was eighteen, I started having my hair cornrowed with extensions. The braider was a friend of a friend, and very good. She worked fast, and didn't make the braids overly tight, although the first time she did my hair, smiling hurt for a week! I remember her because shortly after she started braiding my hair,

I moved to the U.S.A. I was thrilled to learn that the same woman was visiting and staying around the corner from me—at Mr. Boyfriend's home—and she was a friend of his family's. I tried to set up an appointment with her, but it never would "take" and that's when I began to learn two important lessons. 1: People can be very weird and petty; 2: Mr. Boyfriend probably slept with every woman around. I think some men are like that. (Not most men. Some men. I don't know or want to hazard a guess at the proportions, but this is my theory: Some men will always sleep around, and work at doing so. Women probably just fall into bed with other men, and then there are men who pace themselves.) Anyway, Mr. Boyfriend eventually told me that the hairstylist would not do my hair because she liked him! Oh, did I mention that she was married?

Undaunted, I started doing my own hair braiding. I still am not good at cornrows, but I started doing small "box braids"— small plaits to me, but I learned that that's what American women called them. With the perm, the braids were kinda straight; I still have my freshman ID card with that look! But as my hair grew, I trimmed the ends in order to get rid of the chemically treated portion. I had decided that I would wear my hair natural. More than twenty years later, I have never gone back to chemicals.

I wanted to wear my hair natural because it felt good in its natural state. Whenever my roots would grow out, I would sit around and play with the new growth. I enjoyed the waves, the soft texture in contrast to the straight wiriness of the permed hair. And then it occurred to me at eighteen: Why not fully enjoy my own hair? Why do I have to straighten it? Why can't I wear my hair in styles that work with *my* hair texture? There would be no more straight-haired styles. So? I'm not white. White women don't (didn't!) wear their hair braided—Bo Derek notwithstanding— why did I need to wear my hair straight? And I remember thinking: I'm not going to run to straight hairstyles for "special occasions" either! That felt like selling out. It's okay to be me, to look like the Black woman that I am on an everyday basis, but on special occasions, I have to emulate a more white look? No.

I decided that I would not get married with straight hair. Typically, that's the biggest occasion for most of us, and even women who wore braids most of the time would always wear a permed style for major occasions. I decided that I wouldn't do that. And so, on my long, white-dress wedding day I wore my hair braided—parted to one side and flowing with cornrows. I was beautiful! Young and beautiful in a gorgeous dress my mother made and with fresh, flowing cornrows. By then, it was four or five years since I had started to grow my hair out and it was shoulder length. I no longer needed extensions for length, but learned that its texture kept the cornrows tighter and neater for a much longer time than without.

In those days, I was living with Mummy again and she marveled at the thickness and length of my hair each time I unbraided it. Just looking at it seemed to overwhelm her. Me? I managed it fine. I had (re)learned how to take care of it as it grew out of the permed state, bit by bit. It was never a big deal to me. It was the way it was, and I washed and combed it out without any of the trauma of my childhood. As my hair grew even longer, I stopped wearing cornrows with extensions, and went back to doing my own box braids. It was a lot of hair though—long and extremely thick—but most people could not tell because I wore it braided, which I suppose "contained" it. Once, when visiting relatives in Toronto, as I looked through the viewfinder of my camera to take a picture of them, I saw my three aunts giggling and looking rather conspiratorial. When I enquired about the source of their merriment, I learned that one had informed the others that the length of my braids was due to extensions. They were not! And to prove it, as soon as I returned to California, I took a picture in a bikini top, posing with my hair all loosed out and sent it to them!

Once I treated myself with a visit to a New York stylist for a wash and flat iron. As is always the case when my hair is viewed "out" in its natural state, there was a lot of oohing, and awing, and clucking. I wondered whether the stylist would be able to handle my hair, but after an unremarkable washing, I was stunned to see the stylist grab a hair dryer with a comb attachment and head my way. I had never used one of those before! In what seemed like a flash, she had dried my entire head of hair and it was straight! Not white-straight...but my curls were pulled out and my hair was dry. Just like that. No fuss. In very little time! Where was this when I was a child? Why hadn't I heard about this before? Although I was taking care of my hair with relative ease, this was revolutionary! I still tell mothers of Black daughters about this way of drying hair; if I can save one little girl from my childhood experience, the crusade will be worth it!

There are two hairstyles that I had long admired on other Black women: well-kept locks, and being just this side of bald. I always felt that I did not have the courage to cut my hair off. I had worn long hair all the time I knew myself, and the thought of *not* having it was scary. After several years of wearing my box braids, I started longing for locks. I did some "interviewing" of women who had the kind of locks I imagined having and was very disappointed when several such conversations confirmed that they took lots of maintenance. I was looking for a way to look great without any effort. Guess that Holy Grail does not exist! (Where in life does the no effort thing pay off anyway, right?) I put locks back on the shelf.

When I was studying for my doctoral exams, I suddenly had had enough of my hair and wanted it gone. I liked it well enough but just didn't want it on me. I fantasized about getting home from the gym and heading for a shower that started at the top of my head. On July 7, 1994, I decided to just do it. I had never been to a hair salon in the years I had lived in Los Angeles (I wonder how many people living in L.A. could say that?) so I didn't know where to go to get my hair cut. I remembered that my mother went to a salon nearby, so I called and asked whether they had someone who could do a barber cut, and when they said yes, I cut all my braids off, leaving inch and a half stumps around my head. I kept a few of the braids for posterity and hurried over to have my first short cut.

All of the workers in the salon were dismayed upon hearing what I had done, and the African American woman who was to cut my hair refused to cut it all off as I requested. I wanted a buzz cut! She was afraid that it was too drastic to go from hair all my life to a buzz cut and so she promised to cut it "low-ish" and said I could return for a closer cut if I still wanted one after a few days. Cutting my hair off didn't feel at all brave —which is what I thought it took all the years I had been admiring others. It felt pragmatic. It felt right. I was very focused on my exams and the hair was superfluous. I had no extra weight to carry literally or figuratively. I was a gym rat with a buff body. I was a studying machine. I wanted utilitarian hair. I loved having it off! I especially liked wearing it buzzed in the summer. I felt sexy and strong. Powerful. Comfortable in my skin and without a worry about whether men would find me attractive, although I received lots of positive feedback from men and women. Many women expressed a wish for the same hairstyle along with fear and worry about what others (including their mothers) would think. In what remains one of the oddest responses to my new look, a famous Antiguan musician said: "Janis, you got man-head now!" I don't know what his intention was, and never spent time trying to figure it out, but the interaction did teach me that it is possible to travel the world and remain unsophisticated.

I met my current husband, and dated more than I ever had before, with short hair. I think that was less because of my physical appearance and had everything to do to with the self-confidence I exuded — the same confidence that allowed me to finally cut my hair. The one thing I missed about long hair was the ability to change my appearance by wearing a different style. I wore my braids many ways—in updos, partial updos, all down...but even with a great hair cut, that's it! So after almost ten years of short hair, I decided that I would grow my hair again. I was surprised that my husband protested, but I ignored him and after a few failed attempts, during which I would have the barber take all the growth off, I stayed the course. I met another woman who was in the same process and she told me of a product she was using to twist her hair. Now that I was growing it out, I had no idea what to do with hair that length, as I'd never had short hair—other than a styled short cut. Initially, I could not even part my hair because it was so short. Then I remembered the way I had initially started growing my natural hair—with cornrows and extensions—and I asked around to find a suitable place. I recall going to the salon and picking out style after style only to be told that my hair was not long enough.

I mainly wore twists, and before long, my hair was back. Strolling through a mall one day, an Eastern European woman in a kiosk beckoned me over. She was holding a flat iron. I was amused that she thought her iron would work on *my* hair. I went over though, and she went on about the product and how it could be used on any type of hair, wet or dry, and so on. She wanted to try it on my hair, and I wanted to give her the opportunity to fail but was self-conscious because my hair was not freshly washed. So a few weeks later, I washed my hair, put all except for a small section in the back into a ponytail and headed for the kiosk! I was stunned when with one stroke of this magical instrument my hair was bone strait! No grease, no spray, no nothing. And my hair felt sooooft! She did a few sections of the ponytail and showed me how the iron could be used to curl. I said, "Well, you need to do the whole ponytail or I'll look lopsided!" (This was a great way to get a hairdo as I headed off for a date with my husband.) As the saleswoman headed towards me with a spray bottle of water, I felt dismay! She giveth and now she would take it away with that water! She sprayed my hair and then used her magic instrument on that section and sure enough with a hiss and some steam, my hair was bone straight yet again. Now, she had my attention, and I started considering purchasing the gadget. I had gone to the kiosk to be entertained and to show her that the gadget would not work for my hair, but how much were these things? She reeled off prices and deals for the various sizes, but alas, one to three hundred dollars was not going to change hands so that I could play with my hair!

Then I thought of the wonders of eBay, or at least what I had heard of eBay. I had a friend school me on how to use eBay and within days, I had my very own Wet to Dry flat iron! It came just in time for me to wear Christmas hair. It was a blast. I had been noticing that even after washing my hair, it was not returning to its original texture—it was straighter! However, I didn't pay much attention to this until January rolled around and I was ready to get back to my "regular" life.

I washed my hair and twisted it as per usual. Now my twists

were straighter! I found this very annoying and began to feel angry because the flat iron seemed to have robbed me of "my" hair. After a few weeks of trying to figure out what my next move was, I decided that I would cut my hair again. The straight but natural look was fun, but I had intensified my workout program and the thought of coming in from the gym and jumping under the shower with a cap on was not enticing. Surprise to me: My husband was dead set against the haircut. The same man who did not want me to grow it in the first place now did not want me to cut my hair. So, I made a deal with him: I'd wear my hair long if he would take care of it! As a man of his word, he has!

Truthfully, I'm enjoying having long hair again. I'm enjoying it in a new way now that I'm experimenting with the flat iron, and many new products. There are soooo many hair products on the market now, it's mind-boggling. I walked through what looked like a small supermarket yesterday, and every aisle was stocked with hair products—shampoos, conditioners, and mousses. An employee told me that this was only a portion of the products this new mall store would carry. Now we have entire lines that "enhance" curls, others that "slick" hair. More evolution! I had no idea that wearing my hair naturally included all of these options. When I started braiding my hair, I made peace with the idea that braids were my only option. I felt that styling the braids (ponytail, box braids, cornrows, upsweep, and so on) gave me lots of variety. But suddenly, I can go curly or straight or wear my hair "out" without suffering chemicals! There's a whole world of options to explore, if I have enough money, interest, time, and bathroom cabinet storage for the products.

These options are in sync with who I am today. I'm more at

ease in my life...more flexible...more willing to experiment. I don't feel as rigid as I looked, and was, when I had short hair. As symbolized by my hair, I am fun, carefree, and embracing change!

Conversations with
Young Black Women
in Toronto

*...my conclusions from eyewitnessing, listening,
and sometimes listening-in...*

One young Black woman in Toronto who wishes to remain anonymous tells me that she finds herself in a quandary: while she likes wearing her hair in its natural state, she does not dare do so if she hopes to attract a Black man. Until she knows how a man feels about natural hair, she plays it safe and wears her hair straightened, for she believes that Black men in their 30s and 40s assume that women with short, natural hair are lesbians.

She describes the situation thus: "Natural hair, for the most part, has a lesbian connotation, while straight, long hair is considered beautiful. I have had both natural and relaxed hair and the difference in reaction from both men and women told me this. When I was mistakenly thought to be a lesbian and told friends, most of them said it was because I had a very short natural hair style." So she straightens her hair.

In 1990, the play *Afrika Solo* by Djanet Sears was staged in Toronto for the first time.. It is a one-woman show that humorously chronicles a young Black woman's voyage of self-discovery. The story begins in a world where Black people are seen via the media as slaves, servants, or man-eating, savage tribesmen. In this world, beauty is judged by the fairness of your skin or hair, and the straightness of your nose.

Women of all races use extensions and weaves, but for most Black women, the option to grow our hair longer is not always available. Unlike white women and Asian women, most Black women don't have hair that grows beyond a certain length—especially, of course, dark-skinned women. This could not be lost on men, who prefer long hair and who also think that women with dreadlocks are likely to be man-haters, feminists, or lesbians. These are harsh stereotypes to live with, especially if you are young, vulnerable about your self-image, and trying to find love.

I noticed that not many women admit the things that motivate them to continue spending money on the upkeep of weaves and perms. I do know that in many cases, women choose long, flowing tresses—no matter what it costs them. Their decision to do so comes out of the thinking that long hair makes them look "better" or more beautiful...or so that they will be more appealing to men. I suspect that they're not always making choices based on their own sense of style. They're choosing based on society's view of the ideal hair. In particular, they are seeking the approval of Black men. That's what I really think is at the heart of choosing to acquire long hair, at such high cost, and going through such aggravation to look after it.

People of all races in Toronto decide how they are going to categorize Black women based on hairstyle. Black women with short, natural hair are seen as "political," strong, maybe angry, and maybe lesbian. Yet, many Black women choose to wear their hair in its natural state, and ignore the stereotyping. They say that they are glad to walk around with the hair with which they were born. Hearing such affirming sentiments makes me feel that all is not lost. After all, how could it not be "good" hair? Our parents' combined genes provide us with the hair we need.

I spoke with young, Black women who explained that they

wear their hair natural for a time, then at other times, they give in, straighten their hair, and attach a weave that gives them long hair down past their shoulders. This full treatment is done especially if there's a function that is bringing a lot of people together. I am told that women want to make sure that they're always at their "attractive best," and there are only a few guys "out there" who are "into" natural hair.

Some Black women in Toronto stated that sometimes, after years of putting their hair through the straightening process, it becomes severely damaged. At that point, they've been forced to wear their hair in its natural state in order to allow it to regain strength. Some women opt for wigs while their damaged hair is going through the necessary treatments to stop it from breaking and/or falling out. Others add braided extensions, allowing their own hair to rest for anywhere from four to six weeks, at which time they do a fresh set of braids. For some of these women, it will only be a matter of time before they are straightening their hair again. They simply do not feel comfortable wearing their hair in its natural state, given the social milieu in which they do life. For these women, Afros and dreadlocks are out of the question as hairstyle choices, and so wigs are used for the stage in-between healing and renewed growth.

In 2007, Toronto Black women formed an online group called Women for Natural Hair Meet. The group's mandate is: "Meet with other local Black women who choose to wear their hair natural. Gather to commune and support one another in your quest for chemical-free hair! Discuss hair care, maintenance, and the politics of having natural hair." [See *http://naturalhair.meetup.com/cities/ca/on/toronto/*]

In 2007, an American catalogue listing straightening and lengthening hair products promised Black women liberation with these words: "Nothing can boost a woman's self-confidence and attitude more than wearing the hair she always dreamed of but never thought she could have." [Especially Yours® and Specialty Catalog Corp.]

Taija Ryan
(Ms. Ryan is a 22-year-old
Black university student in Toronto)

I think wearing your hair natural is one of those things that you do when you're a kid, then you get to that age where you want to straighten it, wear a weave, and so on. For me, that was not promoted, but I still wanted straight hair. I wanted my own hair, but I wanted it to be straight. It is easier to manage, and it just looks nice.

There is this idea "out there" as you grow up that natural hair is tied to a certain look, or lifestyle, which is you're more like Erykah Badu...the way she dresses...tied to Africa...all that stuff... It's not that you don't want to be tied to Africa, but just not making that "pro-African, pro-natural, pro-Black" statement. For example, if you go for a job interview with natural hair, they might think your natural hair means that you're pro-Africa, and they may not want you in their workplace. They may think that if you feel that strongly about something, then you're a pushy kind of personality, and you're going to be hard to work with. They'll think that everything will have to be politically correct: "We're going to have to watch what we say around her." They may be entirely wrong about the person!

While growing up, you hear "nice hair" meaning straighter hair, and if you have more curly, nappy hair, that means you're more African, and nobody wants that. You hear it from older people, and people's parents. They talk about straight nose, light skin, nice hair. I used to think when I was a kid, "I wish I had white people's hair." I hear little kids say it all the time. They say: "I wish I had white people's hair, it would be so much easier."

I think the whole Black hair thing in Toronto is tied to the roots of the people from the Caribbean and from here. Black people speak of nice, long hair. When you're a child, natural hair is considered cute, but grown-up hair is weaves, straight hair, braids with extensions. Grown-up hair is unnatural hair. I find that weird. Why can't you have natural hair when you're grown-up?

A lot of women feel that natural hair wouldn't attract a man. When they say, "I'm going to get my hair done," they're not going to get natural braids, they're going to get a weave, or straightening, hoping that they'll attract somebody. There is so much focus on the quality of hair. I know some women who say they want to marry and have their children with someone who's light-skinned, so that their children will have "good hair."

Guys say that they hate it when a girl wears weaves; they like girls with natural hair. That's ironic, I think. If some girls only knew that this is what most guys think. Some girls say: "He's just saying that because we're already together. He doesn't want me putting in a weave so that other guys will be attracted to me." But I don't think that's true. I also think that some women believe that guys can't tell that they're wearing a weave. I think that's funny.

My sister and my cousins and my friends tell me a lot about weaves in general; they show me what it takes to maintain: how you put it in, how long it lasts—that type of stuff. Unconsciously, while they're telling me about weaves, they show me why they put them in but it's unconscious. They say things like wanting their weaves to look fresh; they don't want people to see them with their weave/their hair not looking nice. It is as if the hair makes you—if they have a fresh, new weave, then they themselves are fresh...like they're born again. Oh, now I have a ponytail; this is a different side of me. Or: I have new bangs. It's like putting on another disguise. Every time they change it, it's like they change themselves. It's like Superman—every time he takes off the glasses, he becomes Clark Kent. It's ridiculous, but it's sad at the same time. It shows you how much importance is put on the hair, on the weave. There's so much energy going into that when it could be going into different things.

Everyone is contributing—whether they're old, or young, or a kid, they all contribute to this idea that you should have straight hair, or a weave, when you become an adult. There is focus on the colour of the weave, and the style of the weave. I never do a weave, so I'm looked at as a "plain Jane." I just wear my hair straight or natural. When I wear it straight, some people ask me, "Why don't you get a weave?" And when it's natural, some people ask, "Why don't you straighten your hair?"

When I was little, I hated my hair. I had a lot of hair, and it was "tangly," difficult to wash, and difficult to care for. It was not easy at all. It took forever to wash, forever to dry, and forever to braid, and so I never really understood why people were always saying that I had nice hair. They used to say that I had nice hair because it was soft and curly. It was jet-black (because of some Indian in our background), and they also said that it was not "nigger-like." I guess if I was a different kind of person, I might have felt better or superior about it. I think over the years, I grew to love my hair but not because other people liked it.

Some of my friends don't wear weaves all the time, but it's not that they wouldn't get one—for them, it's just a different style. They wear their own hair, and sometimes they get a weave. For them, their natural hair is also just another style, the same Superman thing. For most people, natural hair is just another outfit—a way to change yourself—even though you were born with it.

I know that I would never wear a weave. I think there's just too much energy focused on hair, and most of this energy is focused on constantly changing your hair. A lot of people know how to do weaves, or know someone who can do weaves. So now, it pulls them away from the usual—just going to the hairdresser for a wedding, or something special. Now, everyone does their own weaves, or they do each other's because they want their styles changed too often to be able to go to the hairdresser all the time.

A young Black woman in Toronto, Canada, says: "Some Black men have been conditioned to dislike natural hair on Black women..." Anonymous.

Trey Anthony, African Canadian playwright, author of play, *Da Kink in My Hair*.
Sometimes I've wanted to get rid of the kink in my hair and other times I've loved it and felt glad it was there. [Interview with Shaun Hutchinson in *The New Black Magazine*. London, U.K.]

Black women in the U.K. spend six times more on hair-care products than white women, according to L'Oréal, the French hair and beauty products company.

Maxine Greene
(Ms. Greene is a professional career woman)

Maxine Greene asks: "Why do Black people have to enslave themselves in these discussions about hair? White people do not worry about societal implications of running a flat iron through their hair to make it straight."

She also thinks that she looks more professional with straight hair. "I am already the only Black person in a meeting; I don't want to look more Black." She says of herself ruefully: "I realize that I've been brainwashed." Ms. Greene is not alone in this experience, and this thinking. In Toronto, the marketplace demands a certain appearance, and Black women are ever sensitive to what is required of them going into any venture and to potential strikes against them. Clearly, hair is one large area that requires their assessment, attention, and action.

In 1998, 17-year-old Michelle Barskile of North Carolina was told by her Black sorority, Alpha Kappa Alpha, that because she wore her hair in dreadlocks, she would not be allowed to attend the debutante ball. She was told that if she wished to attend the ball, she would have to pin her dreadlocks up on top of her head...that is, out of sight. Ms. Barskile refused to hide her dreadlocks, even though she had already bought a $500 dress for the event, and thus, did not attend the ball.

Conversations with Mothers of Black Girls

Veronica Ciandre (Toronto, Canada)
...thoughts about natural hair...

My choice in championing natural hair was more personal than political; however, in the early 80s the arc had returned in its slow movement towards where we find ourselves today, with the freedom to choose how to wear one's hair, with less condemnation and fewer questions than we once encountered.

...journey with hair...

I started out with the usual once-a-week ritual of Sunday hair washing. One by one, my two sisters and I had our hair washed, and then spent what seemed like forever in a semi-grip between my mother's knees, screw face at the ready, as she proceeded to sometimes painfully comb, section, oil, and then plait or twist our hair. If your hand went up to protect yourself momentarily from the pain of the combing or the plaiting, it was met by a quick rap on the knuckles with the comb. You had a choice: the hair pain, or the knuckle pain.

Our hair was always well-groomed, and for special occasions tied with the familiar look of matching ribbons in two or three neatly parted sections. We never talked about hair, and I had no reason not to like it.

...hair as statement...

My first request for change came at around age ten. The image of Angela Davis was all over the news, as was her Amazing Afro. I didn't know the politics, but I wore the button that said: "Free Angela Davis." I had no idea what she had done to lose her freedom—if anything. Visions of the raised fist and the words "Black Power" entered my vocabulary at that time. At ten and living in England, I was still on a need-to-know basis, and apparently I didn't need to know why I wanted Angela Davis freed, but I could wear the button nonetheless. What I did know was that her hair was kick-ass-awesome, and that young Black women all over the world were rocking it as a sign of solidarity. I also knew nothing about solidarity but knew I wanted to look solid too.

This was my first lesson in "Hair as Statement," and the fact that it was going to make one for you, whether or not it was the statement you wanted to make. My request was met with a resounding "*no!*" I was not yet old enough to show outward signs of political conviction; I was too young to look like a rebel; I was too young to choose.

My sister, who is three years my senior, was allowed, but my younger sister and I were not. We were considered too young to manage the responsibility, or the protection that might become necessary when one chose to align oneself with rebels. We were not allowed to become rebels. We were too young. We were not allowed to wear the outward signs of the revolution. We were too young.

Born at the beginning of the 60s, I remember vividly that I spent years in the same combination of hairdos. By the time we were given permission to wear an Afro, the political statement had less of a sting. With the Jackson 5 as the inspiration, permission was granted.

This is when I remember learning the term "good hair," or soft hair. For me, all that meant was that achieving an Afro was going to require a bit of finagling, and would require re-finagling at least once every 24 hours. Getting it to stay in that perfect sphere without going flat on top was the challenge of the day, but one I was up for. Soft hair I understood, but what was so good about it?

...straightening black women's hair while wearing natural hair...

I've been a licensed hair stylist since 1981, and in all that time I've only straightened one head of hair. I came to Toronto in 1981, immediately after receiving my license. Azan's was the first Black hair salon in which I worked.

When I was a young girl, my mother didn't allow us to straighten our hair, so I had managed to reach young adulthood quite naturally. I arrived in Toronto and was exposed to so many more Black people, all of whom had their hair well-straightened and blowing in the wind. The old hair fantasies returned. I was now free to choose, and I chose to have it done. The first time was an unpleasant experience. I had to rinse the relaxer off before the suggested time because it was burning so much. The hair on my temples thinned out considerably, and it hurt for days. Weeks later I had the roots redone, and the experience was no different. That was the end of my relationship with straightening my hair.

When I returned to Vancouver, I was invited by a friend in Seattle, Washington, to come down and work in their hair salon. I was offered the job mostly because of my newly gained experience working with chemically relaxed/straightened hair. It was for the most part a salon for natural hair but it had a few clients whose hair was either chemically relaxed, or blown out, or hot combed. These are all other techniques for getting the hair to look straight. I loved the work they were doing on natural hair, and I told them quite clearly that I wanted to do what they did. When I left the salon four months later, I was no longer styling relaxed hair, and my straight hair was now in braids.

I returned to work at a popular salon in Yorkville and informed them that I did not want to chemically straighten anyone's hair. What they told me was that I would not be able to earn any money without the added charge of the chemical relaxer and straightening the hair by whatever means. So initially I braided at home on the weekends. Soon I was booking up to four clients a week. At this point, I was offered a chair in the salon, just for braiding. I opted to keep the clients at home, rather than take the business to the salon.

I had proved rather quickly that I could earn quite a good living without having to straighten hair. The deal was if it required much more than water and oil, then I didn't do it at home. I had come this far, and managed to straighten only one head of hair.

Fall – 2007 – *Glamour* Editor to Lady Lawyers: Being Black is Kinda A Corporate 'Don't'. The latest issue of *Glamour* magazine advizes readers to use "Kimble Leave-in Conditioner" followed by a flat iron, and a curling iron, followed by spritzer and augmented with hair extensions to achieve "Mary J. Blige's loose, beautiful curls."

...hair reaching for the sky...

My daughter spent her first three years running from anything to do with combing her hair. Most of the time I groomed her hair when she was asleep. Amazingly, at about four, she sat for three hours and allowed her hair to be fully cornrowed; from then on the idea of grooming sunk in.

At around age five, she was often told that she and her hair looked like Scary Spice. The only part that she remembered at the time was "scary," since she didn't know who the Spice Girls were. The texture of her hair was very much like a baby's for a long time. When she made the observation that it would never lie down, I compared the weightlessness to fairy hair and said that it was always reaching for the sky. She liked that.

After seeing a cousin with fully blown out hair at about age seven, she asked if she could have the same done to her hair. I simply said, "No," explaining that it wasn't necessary. I also told her it was usually done when someone wanted to make the hair more manageable (not prettier), and that her hair was easy enough to manage.

I remember being afraid that if I straightened her hair once, she would never get over it and would spend a good part of her days pining for something I wouldn't allow.

At age eight, she asked again, and I agreed to blow out both her hair and my niece's hair for that Christmas Day. I warned them not to think this was going to be a regular occurrence, and that it was time-consuming and high maintenance (as they would later see for themselves). I also said that both of them had hair that was beautiful as it was. It was interesting to watch the difference it seemed to make to their confidence; it was as if they became more animated. I simply observed and let them know that I loved their curly hair more.

My daughter's straight hair lasted about a week. She was happy to have her curly hair back and appreciated the low maintenance of it. About two years later, she asked for it again for a school picture. By then, she had not only grown to love and appreciate her hair but she had also mastered the ability to groom it herself in a variety of ways. I had also braided her hair myself a number of times, as well as taking her to a local hair-braiding salon—all of which she thoroughly enjoyed.

At this point I was confident that she appreciated her hair enough, and there was little threat of her wanting it to be straight permanently. I also didn't want her to want it more because I had said no. We blew out her hair for "picture day," and after a week of seriously trying to maintain it, she joyfully allowed the curls to come back. She expressed relief and appreciation once again for her natural hair.

From a very young age, I have always been conscious of the words I use to describe everything to do with her hair...never using words to suggest any difficulty or disapproval. I wanted her to know that her hair was beautiful, long before she heard anything suggesting otherwise. My allowing her to blow out her hair on occasion has actually decreased her desire to have straight hair. It is no longer a mystery to her.

Skira Martinez, mother of two daughters (Ontario, Canada)
...relaxed about my daughters' hair...
I went to elementary school in a small town in Northern Ontario. I was teased a lot by the other children. I was the only Black child in my class. When the snow fell and it hit the white girls' hair, it fell, but it stayed on mine and my two younger sisters'. When I

was older and came to Toronto, other Black people said I had good hair, but I didn't feel that way about my hair. In Northern Ontario, I was considered dark; in Toronto, I was considered light. The only thing that I wanted to change was my hair. I wanted hair that could move, that I could flip over my shoulder, hair that would blow in the wind.

When I was younger, we lived in the country on a small farm. We had a copper comb that you could heat and run through your hair to straighten it. When I discovered that comb, I was in heaven. Later on, I had it relaxed when I moved to live in Toronto.

My own experience with hair made me relaxed about my daughters' hair. When they wanted their hair straightened, I was comfortable about it because I understand that it has something to do with confidence. At some point I hope that they will love their own natural hair, but banning them from changing their hair texture might do more harm than good. I think one day they will wear their natural hair proudly. I point out how beautiful natural hair is, and I do so as casually as I can. A number of singers have started to wear their hair natural, and I like to point that out to them as well. I'm glad that they are in an environment that's different from the one I grew up in—I'm very glad of that—so they see people who look like them and have hair like them.

Once I moved out of the small Northern Ontario town, and was around more Black people, I felt like I was accepted for who I was and what I looked like. My hair was no longer odd or strange; so many other people had hair like mine. I stopped straightening my hair, and everyone around me was supportive about it, especially women. Some men commented that they preferred my hair the way it was before.

The general white public responds to my hair being out and curly as if they think I'm radical, or am overly confident. It is as if they think I am a strong Black woman because of my natural hair. They are intimidated by it; they see it as confidence. There are a few Black people who think that if your hair is natural then you're letting yourself go, but that thinking doesn't affect me. Those people who are close to me and know me do not have that response. Where it does affect me is in terms of employment. I can remember once a potential employer asked me if I could tie my hair back.

Elaine Nash and daughters, Nina and Raina
(Atlanta, U.S.A.)
...earliest memory of hair...

When I was a child in Antigua, my hair was thick but it wasn't long; when I went to live in St. Croix and my diet included more protein, my hair grew. It was a nutritional problem but I didn't realize that. Everyone around me had the same kind of hair that I had, and so hair was not an issue for me. My mother had moved to live in St. Croix, while we lived with my aunt in Antigua.

My aunt washed my hair and hated doing it because I made a lot of noise. I had a fear of water coming in my face; it felt like I was going to drown...it was terrifying, as the water would come into my eyes. She gave me a rag to hold over my eyes but the soap seeped in. I would scream, and beg for it to stop. She would give me a couple of thumps in my back to get me to keep quiet but I made more noise. She held my head forward, and poured water over my head.

I hated having my hair washed. I was tender-headed, and when my aunt combed out the knots it made me cry; so then she would hit me on my hand with the comb. My aunt had four heads to comb—our two cousins', my sister's, and mine—so it must have been tiring. Whenever I heard, "Time to wash your hair," I would wish I could just get my hair cut off.

When I went to live with my mother in St. Croix at age ten, the drama ended. My mother straightened my hair every two weeks, and pulled it back in a ponytail. The hair drama was over.

...peer pressure...

My oldest daughter had allergies to the milk in baby formulas but we didn't know it at the time; we just knew that after nursing her, she could not tolerate the baby formulas. As she grew older, she began to drink milk, as we were still not aware that she was allergic to it. Then suddenly, her hair began to break. I didn't know what to do: it was brittle and wouldn't grow. The other children in her elementary school—especially the boys—teased her about her hair. So we tried a Jheri curl, and the children then called her "Jheri curl juice," so we soon let that grow out. We went to perming it, thinking that maybe this would help, but the perm broke off her hair. So then she went to extensions.

The kids in school had a focus on straight hair, and I think she received a lot of peer pressure. I think she believes that her hair *makes* her. Besides peer pressure, I think it came from the fact that three of her friends were bi-racial, and perhaps in her view, they exemplify beauty. It is the same beauty standard that you see in magazines, on television, in people such as Beyoncé and Mary J. Blige—that's the standard.

She says that she would get bored with natural hair, but I think she believes that people wouldn't think she looked good with her natural hair. Understandably, she wants to fit in, and I think that she believes that straightened hair and weaves are fashionable.

...embraces natural hair ...

My younger daughter's hair was long and healthy, as there was no allergic reaction with which to contend. She is into natural things, so she has had a different experience with peer pressure. She used to perm her hair but stopped. Now, she embraces natural hair; she is a hairdresser of natural hair only. She uses extensions but does not straighten her hair any more.

Raina, younger daughter of Elaine Nash (Atlanta, U.S.A.)
(30-plus, African American woman;
works as a hair stylist of natural hair)
...journey with my hair...

In the tenth grade I wanted locks (dreadlocks), but my mom said I needed to be established in a career before selecting that hairstyle. Natural hair has been more acceptable in the last ten years.

The majority of women at college had natural hair. [They were] an unusual group of women, very conscious, into writing, a whole different vibe than the girls I was used to. They made it comfortable for me to feel that in going natural, I would have a support system. Eventually, I "locksed" my hair; it was a personal growth experience.

I became more in tune with myself, my whole being, including my physical being.

I went through a drastic change in my diet. I stopped eating meat; I still eat fish. I became more open-minded, even in terms of religion. I drifted from Christianity to connect with myself inside, and I became spiritually conscious. It made a deep enough impact that I started being more into natural hair, and made it my career choice. I set limits: I won't do fake locks, and I don't straighten hair. I want Black women to become more accepting of their natural being.

I notice that men with dreadlocks do not necessarily give me a second look, and they tend to be with lighter-skinned women who don't have locks. One thing I've noticed is that locks have become "crazy-popular" among unemployed, young Black men, and perhaps that's giving locks a bad name.

I used to volunteer with Black kids, and they were very narrow-minded about hair; they had the whole "good hair/bad hair" judgement. They considered natural hair to be nappy, kinky, and other negative words. They were brainwashed to think that straight hair was better, especially because their hair hurt to be combed. They don't understand that the comb is a European thing. Most of their moms permed their hair really early, and so these children came to believe that something was wrong with their natural hair.

I am the only one in the salon in which I work who does natural hair, and there is always this line drawn between me and the women who do perms. They're very into weaves; they wear them all the time and are not comfortable with their natural hair. They're into creating some other person that they're not naturally. Bob Marley's kind of locks are not accepted as much as other kinds of locks, the kind that are considered more fashionable, less Rasta-looking. Because I colour my locks, they are thought of as looking more modern—less Rasta in people's minds.

Nina, elder daughter of Elaine Nash (Atlanta, U.S.A.) (30-plus, African American woman) ...natural, straight, curly, twists...

I love different hairstyles. I love my sister's dreadlocks, and I love my mom's hair. She's just wearing it natural, and I wear different styles: natural, straight weaves, curly weaves; sometimes it has colour in it; sometimes I wear braids; and sometimes I wear twists.

...some negative reactions to my natural hair...

When I wear my hair natural, some people—usually young Black women—look at my natural head as if they're smelling doo-doo. Most of my friends use perms. They don't really care when I wear my hair natural; some of them tell me that it suits me better. They're pretty supportive of my wearing my hair natural. They're somewhat proud of me because it's not the norm to have a natural in America. They're proud that I step outside of the box and stick with it.

I haven't had a perm since 2005; getting to that point took me some time. My hair had started breaking. At one point in time I would have cared when people made negative comments, like "nappy head," but as I've got older, I've come to a point where I don't care what anybody says about my hair.

I think perming my hair changed the texture of my hair. I've decided that when I have children I will not perm their hair, even if it's very coarse. I think having your hair natural gives you a certain sense of pride. We went to a majority white school, and I think that I wanted my hair permed because I wanted to be more like everybody else.

...different treatment, depending on hairstyle...

I decided to do an experiment and wear my natural hair for a week to see how many people would come up and say something to me. Then I wore extensions and compared the reactions. I got more attention when I had my extensions in. More people come up to me to have conversations with me when I had a weave. When I wear a natural I attract fewer men, and they're usually wearing dreadlocks.

There was a time when I thought I wouldn't wear my hair natural because I knew that guys don't go for girls with nappy hair;

then I decided to just do what I wanted with my hair. I have a friend who thinks that guys won't take to women with natural hair, and that they'll think she looks like a boy.

I do know that some women are hesitant about going natural. If they're in a relationship, they think the man might leave, and if they don't have a relationship, they think they won't attract a man. It seems to be prevalent with Black men that women have long, straight hair—whether it's extensions, or weaves—they are just not attracted to women with natural hair. If a woman has long, natural hair she still has no chance...it can't be nappy. I noticed that girls with naturals did not get dates. One guy told me that he needs to run his fingers through his woman's hair. He said: "I don't want to put my hand in a woman's hair and get stuck."

...boys in high school...

I wore my hair short and permed in high school and no boys liked me. Another girl who had short, permed hair had the same experience. There were a couple of people with whom I was really close: one was mixed with white and Black, the other one had a perm but her hair was long. I remember feeling inferior to them because of their hair. I remember wishing my hair could be long, or look like their hair; it was really tough for me.

When I got out of high school, I happened to also have a group of friends who all had long hair as well, and for a long time I didn't like going out with them. I felt as if people were wondering why I was with them. It took me a while to become confident with who I am, and to accept myself, my hair, my beauty. My hair is nappy hair. It is who I am, take it or leave it.

Young Black women will notice that in the media—in TV shows, in music videos—the girls in the videos and shows don't look like you. And you're so young, just in elementary school, or middle school, and you think, "Oh, I must not be pretty." Even now, when you watch television shows, you don't see a lot of women with natural hair. As you get older and read more, you will find women who are empowered, who have natural hair, but usually on TV your favourite singer doesn't look like you. So, role models are good outside of the home; someone besides your mom who lets you know that you're okay as you are.

When I had a perm, there was one guy who asked me if I'd ever thought about wearing a natural. He said that he liked women who wear naturals. It was surprising to me because I was used to guys liking perms. He even suggested braids or some other way of looking more natural.

April 2006. Susan L. Taylor, Executive Editor of *Essence Magazine* learned that a department at Hampton University in Virginia, a historically Black university, had a strict, no-braids, no dreadlocks policy for its students. She promptly cancelled a speaking engagement with the university, and issued the following statement:

"I recently withdrew my participation in the 28th Annual Conference on the Black Family at Hampton University. It has always been important for me to honor my commitments, so I feel it's imperative to explain my actions. I began receiving E-mails from numerous sources advising me of disturbing regulations disallowing locks and braided hairstyles for Hampton students. One such e-mail included an Associated Press story headlined: 'University Bans Certain Hairstyles for Students.' As a businesswoman and public figure who has proudly worn my hair braided for more than 25 years, I was incredulous and felt insulted. My executive assistant, Debra Parker, contacted the university for clarification, and when she was advised that this was the school's policy, I easily made the decision to cancel my visit.

I strongly recommend that you reconsider this policy and invite informed image consultants to address students in your business program about how to make individual style work in the corporate environment. Perhaps the greatest challenge your students will face in the work world is remaining whole and true to themselves in environments that are often hostile to

African Americans. Staying connected to our community and culture is critical. Trying to transform themselves to fit into hardly welcoming environments has scarred countless numbers of Black people."

Andrea Oliver, mother of one daughter (London, U.K.)
...first feelings about my hair...

Yes, well now...*hair*...it's such an emotive word! I always had, and sometimes still have, a vestige of shame about my hair or lack thereof! My father had very strong ideas about what a Black woman's hair should look like, and mine never even came close.

I have, and have always had, the kind of hair that I can only describe as weak and flimsy. You can't straighten it (horror of horrors!), you can't dye it, and it breaks off at the sides if you pull it up too tightly, too regularly. So I had years of trying to force it to do all kinds of things that just made it, and me, very unhappy. Then, as a teenager, I got eczema in my head, and my hair fell out. It was a mortifying experience, not helped by my father looking at me with thinly veiled disgust (and, weirdly, also anger?). He asked me if I'd rather stay inside so no one could see me.

After the trauma of that experience with eczema, my hair did happily grow back, and I discovered that cane rows (same as cornrows) really were the way forward. This may seem like an odd statement...but growing up in the 70s as the only Black girl in a massive British comprehensive school meant that wearing cane rows to school was an act of bravery! I was sent to talk to the headmistress about it because I had got Mum to put beads in too and was told that it just not acceptable. To cut a long story short, I fought them, and of course I won!

When my daughter was born with a full head of glorious hair, I am afraid that I was hurled back to my days of shame as a young girl, and the phrase "good hair" leapt into my mind! I actively had to refrain from playing with her hair all the time when she was small because I finally had a head of hair of which I could be proud!

These days I am once more growing my hair back after shaving it all off a couple of years ago, when once more, it was in a bit of a state after being attacked by eczema.

I have since found a wonderful friend who is a kind of dread (dreadlocks) natural hairdresser, Leslie-Ann, and she has managed to nurse my poor, beleaguered hair back to health.

...care of daughter's hair...a smooth journey...

My daughter and I have had a kind of checkered relationship around her hair. Like most children, she hated having it done but still wanted it to look nice; so, what with both my daughter and me being of the fiery variety, we did *fight!* I used to sometimes almost have to sit on her just get it into two pigtails. Then when she hit her looking-in-the-mirror or vanity years, it was with great sadness that I watched her decide she needed it to be straight.

I have always tried to show her the beauty of her natural hair, but the voice of one mother against the entire MTV network (my daughter is a TV host) is a tiny and insignificant sound indeed... . So I have watched her straighten it, weave it—do everything to it, except to just leave it be—but I guess one day she'll work it out for herself. As far as my own hair is concerned, I have finally realized that it is like every other part of my body, it needs love and tender care, and then it will thrive! And as for the eczema, you know the score: no dairy, no wheat, no sugar...and I sometimes think, what? *No fun!*

...sharing my journey with my daughter...

One story that sticks out for me is another school moment. I had plucked up the courage to wear cane rows to school, and Mum had put in silvery white beads all along the fringe. I was so excited; I finally felt pretty. I walked into my German class and my teacher exclaimed to the whole class: "*Mein Gott, wass is dass?*" (My God, what is that?) He stood at the front of the class, pointing and laughing at me. Of course, the whole class then joined in, and I stood at the door waiting for the earth to swallow me up, or lightning to strike me, or hopefully him! When he managed to calm down, I took my seat, shaking with fury, and hurt, and embarrassment.

I did share stories like this one with my daughter, sometimes just because we were talking, and sometimes in a conscious attempt to help her to navigate her way to understanding her own beauty. I really don't know how effective that was; it just made her want to protect me from what she would always call "angry men." In some ways I feel that we've grown up together, she and I. When I had her, I was twenty years old, and really did think I was a big grown woman (ha!), so sometimes we have been learning simultaneously, I think. Personally I am so much more happily inhabiting my own *entire* body, including my hair, and that means that I am stronger for her in every way. I have more for her to draw on when she needs to do so.

I have extension twists in my hair now, and every few weeks I take them out and comb my hair, and put oil in it, and then tuck it back away to grow it but I don't feel like I'm hiding it. I feel like I'm giving it the protection it needs from this cold and chilly place. It's like a flower that can't take the wind and the frost, so I have to wait for the proper climate to let it out!

My lovely hairdresser friend, Leslie-Anne, has me drinking this fabulous tea that is a mixture of horsetail, nettle, and rosemary. I buy them loose from the health food shop...horsetail is naturally occurring silica, which is what hair, skin, and nails are partially made up of, so it really does promote growth and health for all of those areas. It combines two parts horsetail, one and a half parts nettle, and one part rosemary. I make it twice a day in a lovely china teapot; it's a very soothing ritual.

As I grow healthier and strong, so does my hair (really!). So maybe all that time it was weak and flimsy and breaking because so was I? My daughter is 23 now, and I can see her becoming more forgiving and more loving to her own self. Her hair is still straight though, and I long for the day when she comes to my door in all of her curly, wild-haired beauty.

An interesting twist: a case in the U.K.

In 2005, a white 13-year-old schoolgirl, Olivia Acton, returned to school from a holiday in the Canary Islands with her hair braided in cornrows. The head teacher of her school summarily dismissed the child, stating that her braided hair did not conform to the school's code of dress. When pressed to explain how it was that two other pupils of African Caribbean background were allowed to attend school with their hair in braids, the head teacher explained that it was within their cultural and ethnic heritage. Olivia was told: "It's not your culture."

The head teacher further explained that "street culture" was not allowed in the school, but that some leeway was made for the cultural and ethnic background of the children. Cornrows were not part of Olivia's culture, thus if she returned to school wearing them, she would have to stay on her own in the "learning support unit."

Olivia Acton's father wanted to take the case to court, but the MP for the area worked at having the school's governing body mediate a compromise, as he felt that the family have a genuine complaint. An education spokesperson agreed, saying that the school ought to focus on what goes into the students' heads, rather than what is on their heads.

[Originally reported in the *Guardian* newspaper Friday, March 18, 2005.]

Glenda Prince, mother of two daughters
(Austin, Texas, U.S.A.)

...first thoughts about hair...

Ever since I was a little girl, hair has always been an issue for me. When I was five years of age, my mother would send me to Miss Maize to have my hair pressed, or fried, or hot-combed. People have used each of these words, depending on their take on the whole idea. This process takes a lot of time, and actually involves using a "pressing comb" and "pressing oil." Sometimes it results in burns to the head, depending on the experience and skill of the person doing the pressing.

At such a tender age, Mommy would wash my hair, and use the vacuum cleaner (I kid you not) to dry it. Let me just explain! This was 1964 in British Guiana, where having a hair dryer was unheard of. Being the improviser that she was, Mommy would turn the nozzle in the opposite direction, so that instead of sucking up air, it would blow out cool air in order to dry the hair. After the drying process, I would more than likely have an appointment with Miss Maize who would spend about two hours "pressing" my hair. Back then my hair was long enough for Mommy to braid or plait it; and my two side-plaits were long enough for me to tie them in a knot under my chin.

...pressing/ironing Hair...

When I was a little older I graduated to having cornrows done in my hair by my cousin Rhonda. The cornrows were perfect since I played netball (basketball) and needed to have a hairdo that would last for at least a month without my having to do anything with it. The hair-plaiting process was a *longish* one but well worth it since the braids lasted for such a long time, and we could wash the hair with the cornrows still in place.

In the mid-80s, the Afro was very popular, and I cut off my hair and sported a cute little Afro for about five years until permed hair became fashionable. Then I had my hair permed. With permed hair, you can spend many hours sitting at the hair salon, and then have to roller set your hair if you want it to be stylish the following day. In addition to this, constantly putting chemicals into your hair can eventually cause breakage and damage the hair.

I remember going to parties with cousins in England and getting home at around five a.m. to grab a few hours sleep only to have to set my hair in rollers before going to bed. Wearing your hair permed is very debilitating; you are almost a prisoner of your hair. You have to have it touched up every six weeks, and roller set every night in order for it to have some bounce. And there is a small chance that if someone who is inexperienced works on your hair, you can get burned from the chemicals that are contained in the cream.

...afro...

After experimenting with different hairstyles, I decided—about fourteen years ago—to just wear my hair natural and as close as possible to my scalp. I remember going to the barber shop and saying to the barber: "Just cut it off." It was that serious. It was also liberating.

The only drawback with wearing my hair in a low Afro in Austin, Texas, is that Black men do not appreciate Black women with their hair this short. On more than one occasion, I have been asked to grow it back, or been told outright that I am not attractive with my hair this short. White men, on the other hand, think my hair is very attractive, and very sexy. Go figure!

India.Arie sums it up nicely: "I am not my hair, I am not my skin, I am the soul that lives within." That is what I am. A beautiful woman with short hair. And a beautiful soul within.

...long hair and acceptance...

Imagine my horror when my eldest daughter, upon entering high school, decided that she wanted to wear her hair permed. I believe that it is all about being accepted at school. For Black girls, there is something about long hair and acceptance—the longer the hair, the more you fit in.

Recently here in the U.S.A., African American women have been adding extensions to their own hair. This not only adds body and length to their hair but also makes it more versatile. Hair can then be worn up or down, or in a ponytail with these extensions, whereas if you have short hair, you are limited to one style. The one thing I like about extensions is that the natural hair is braided into cornrows, and then the extensions are sewn onto the cornrows. This serves as another way of giving the natural hair a break from combing and plaiting.

...healthy, strong, and perm-free...

By the age of ten, my youngest daughter was very involved in several sports, and so as to accommodate this very busy lifestyle, I decided to perm her hair. My reasons were based on convenience, and not style. I was fully aware of the pitfalls perming her hair at such a young age but I went ahead anyway.

During her basketball, or soccer, or track training sessions, her hair gets soaked with perspiration. Not being able to wash out the perspiration after each session, she would just go straight to bed. After months of doing this, her hair started breaking...the damage had already been done. We tried conditioning and putting the hair in braids to stall this breakage but to no avail. Finally about a year ago, I decided: No more! No braids! No perms! Nothing!

I trimmed her hair to get the perm out of it, and I started twisting it with gel. Her hair finally started growing, and the quality has returned to the way it was when she was a toddler—healthy and strong and perm-free. And a bonus is that she is very proud of her natural hairstyles.

Itah Sadu, mother of one daughter (Toronto, Canada)
...childhood memories of hair...

When I was growing up in Barbados, people said I had "good hair." When I was a child, there were different types of hair. There was knotty hair, short hair, bad hair, and of course, good hair. Due to a slight mixture in my phenotype, I ended up with "good hair." This meant that I had thick, shoulder-length, heavy, smooth hair. In fact, people would refer to me as "the child with good hair" and my grandmother took pride in dressing my hair daily.

On special occasions, I was sent to Miss Baird, the hairdresser, to have my good hair made better—which meant that she pressed and hot-combed my hair to look like white people's hair. At other times, the teenage girls in my neighbourhood braided my hair in cornrows with the hot, new, and latest styles. In fact, the daily grooming of hair played a major role in my deportment. The era of colonialism, the impact of enslavement, the dominant images of whites in picture books, coupled with the countless white dolls with blonde hair that were available resulted in my yearning for better hair...no...the *best* hair: blonde hair.

I spent many days wearing a white or yellow towel on my head, flicking it around in the mirror, while marveling at its length and bounce. I wanted bangs, pigtails, and ponytails, just like the girls I saw in the books, and so I treated my white dolls with great care and love, while I spanked the Black dolls. I spanked them, not only because they were Black, but also because they did not have good, golden, blonde, silky, flowing hair.

...thick, wavy hair...

As a person of African descent, I have always been interested in and fascinated by discussions about the politics of hair—in particular, the politics of hair and African/Black women and children. When I became a mother, I sought to identify my daughter's relationship with hair. My daughter has been blessed with a head of thick, wavy hair. In fact, during her infancy, much to my annoyance, people remarked on what "nice/good hair she has."

On April 4, 2007, Don Imus, shock jock of the airwaves, referred to the Rutgers women basketball players as "nappy-headed hos" and "bitches" on his nationally syndicated radio program. Several members of the team are African American, while some of the women are white. Interestingly, all of the African American team members wore their hair straightened.

Imus became the target of heated protests. Kia Vaughn, one of the members of the team, sued him for slander and defamation of character in the State Supreme Court in the Bronx on the day that Imus, who was fired after his comments, settled with CBS Radio. At the time of his firing, his contract pre-empted his threatened $120 million breach-of-contract lawsuit against CBS.

Embodying the Hair on Our Heads

...versions of hair: good hair...
bad hair...coarse hair...nappy hair...

It is interesting to me to hear the ways in which women of African descent identify and are identified by their hair. I have heard all of these, and more: good hair, bad hair, hard hair, coarse hair, picky head, man-head, bald-head, tough hair. At least, those are the terms with which I am most familiar, and I have only listed those that are rooted in my own Antiguan culture...at least those which I know. There are many more negative and positive descriptors for Black women's hair. The most common one I have heard in North America is "nappy." I am quite certain that if I carried out a mini-survey, I could bore myself and the reader with many more of these judgemental ways of describing Black people's— and especially Black women's — hair. The texture, the style, and sometimes even a category goes into the definition. In this essay, I revisit some tales about that categorizing in order to discuss ways of reclaiming our perceptions about our hair.

Several incidents have occurred concerning Black people and hair that have seared their way into the front burner of my consciousness. This is because they are all so incomprehensible to me. The story of Michelle Barskile, discussed above, is particularly sad. The thought of a group of Black women running a sorority and deeming dreadlocks unacceptable was mind-numbing to me.

I was equally shocked when Black mothers of children in a school in New York objected to Carolivia Herron's children's book *Nappy Hair* being read to their children by a white teacher. They were so vociferous in their charge of racism that the teacher was moved from the classroom and put to work in the office. She was later reinstated but has since transferred to another school.

The outcome of these incidents is not my focus—rather, I am concerned about the fact that they occurred in the first place! I believe these two incidents inspired me to one day explore the connections between Black women's self-esteem and their hair. Some later events sealed it for me, but I will come to those later. These first two incidents sent me to revisit "the clime" in which comfort with my natural hair was born. Did I ever not have it? Why did I straighten my hair when I did? What made me stop straightening my hair?

The more I thought about the politics of Black women's hair, the more puzzled I became about the precise reasons that had catapulted so many women to fervently embrace the mainstream standards about hair. Given the power and strength and pride in hair that Black people had journeyed through, and climbed up out of, it made no sense that Black women were still so caught up with hair: good hair, bad hair, kinky hair, nappy hair—the whole mess of words and phrases and insults. Not only had things not seemed to have changed, my gut and my lived, walking reality said that they were worse than ever. And I may never quite understand just why this happened, if it did, and just what "it" is. I am engaged in looking at it through my own eyes...without any "psychologistic" posturing, without any assumptions about radical or reactionary politics. There is more than a simple, neat explanation for why things happen.

So here we are, moving into the twenty-first century, and it seems that not only does Black women's hair continue to be one of their major preoccupations, but the wider society has also begun to focus publicly on Black women's hair. At the same time, Black women increasingly hand out judgements on themselves and on each other based on their hair.

I read with a little ripple of delicious interest the comments that Black women in the U.S.A. made on public forums when Angelina Jolie chopped off her Ethiopian adopted daughter's hair. I say "chopped off" because that is the description that was being used. As one blogger commented: one day the child had a full head of hair, and the next, it was all gone. A number of people wanted to know why the child's hair was not being properly groomed, that is, twisted and moisturized. Several comments were about gender identification, and the issue of having a little girl with such "short hair." One person noted that the child had a full head of hair before she was adopted but now looks like a boy. The most heart-rending cry was: "Why cut off her hair? She's a girl!"

The comments regarding hair-grooming were particularly interesting to me because they indicated how these women interpret the yardstick of beauty. I doubt that Angelina Jolie and Brad Pitt had any idea that for some people their two-year-old daughter's hair was of critical importance to her identity.

Contributors to the discussion seemed to be divided into two camps: one group maintained that the Jolie-Pitts needed to learn to care for the child's hair with combing, moisturizing, braiding, and other grooming techniques, while the other insisted that since the child was of Ethiopian descent, her hair texture didn't need anything more than a comb.

One comment, however, was different from all of the others in terms of acceptance of natural hair:

> *For all these people talking about "do her hair" what the hell y'all talking bout? She is a baby, a little girl...why must she have her hair slicked up?*
> *I bet y'all are the ones who will throw a relaxer in a five-year-old child's hair, and then wonder why her hair won't grow, why it falls out in patches, and breaks off constantly. So dumb! Black hair is Black hair and ain't nothing wrong with it!*

This way of Black women's identities being all tied up in their hair is not a new thing; it is a centuries-old preoccupation, especially on this side of the Atlantic...in North and South America. It goes farther back than Topsy, and it is not something that is going to just go away on its own. Wouldn't it be wonderful if all Black women and girls lived their hair-lives casually? What a wonderful world that would be! No kidding...

...black consciousness...

It is clear that the current mass consciousness of Black people is very different from what it was thirty years ago. That is to be expected. Nothing, and no one remains static. What is a surprise, and maybe even a shock, however, is that it now appears to be far more firmly locked into white consciousness surrounding beauty—the yardstick of mainstream hegemony. It is possible that soon Black parents will once again tell their sons and daughters when they are selecting a spouse: "Put some milk in your coffee." The focus being—as it was when that directive was created—the product from such unions. If a dark-skinned person marries "up"—that is he or she marries someone who is a shade, or several shades, lighter than themselves—then the offspring stand a chance of having "good hair." This is only one of the items on the list of physical characteristics (such as a light skin colour and European facial features) that are highly rated on society's beauty yardstick.

I am not providing new information; this is old stuff—the kinds of things that I have read about, heard about as a teenager, and experienced throughout my adult life. I am setting things in context. We do not have total recall, as Spike Lee reminded us about some of the shifts that have taken place. He devoted his early films to reminding his generation about the power of defining oneself from within. He showed that buying into the standard leads to disempowerment in Black people's lives.

Indeed, for many Black people, these beliefs and attitudes had shifted to a large extent during the Black cultural revolution of the 60s and 70s. In 1968, when James Brown intoned, "Say it loud—I'm Black and I'm proud," it became an anthem for Black people because they were ready to live it. One year later, in Trinidad, The Mighty Duke (Kelvin Pope) won the Calypso King competition with the song "Black is Beautiful." And also in 1969, Nina Simone released a new single, in which she belted out from her gut: "To be young, gifted, and Black!" The music speaks with the voice of the times. So too does the art, dance, clothes, poetry, stories, books, writing, the doing, the feeling, the b-e-i-n-g.

I suspect that those who went through this understanding—

this period of enlightenment—assumed that the enlightened condition would be permanent for everyone then, and for future generations of African peoples. There was no question in my own mind that the power felt in having natural hair would carry over to the next generation—the children of those who had gone through the process of moving from shame and the hot-iron comb to natural hair.

When Zahra Redwood, 25, was crowned "Miss Jamaica" in 2007, she became the first Rastafari woman to hold that title. Women with dreadlocks are rarely seen in beauty contests. Redwood does not just wear the hairstyle, she is a member of the Rastafari religious movement that began in Jamaica in the 1930s.

In 2007, the United Progressive Party government of Antigua and Barbuda, in the Caribbean, prohibited the wearing of hair weaves and hair extensions by children in elementary and secondary schools.

... Jennifer Lopez and Beyoncé Knowles...

The bad news is that the celebratory attitude about *Africanness ...Blackness* did not make the transition on its way to the next generation. In fact—and even notwithstanding the general populace's preoccupation with and celebration of Jennifer Lopez's and Beyoncé Knowles's ample proportions in the gluteus maximus—*Africanness...Blackness* seems to have left in its wake a much more firm commitment to the white mainstream standards of beauty, especially those that govern hair.

There have always been Black women in popular culture who were as amply proportioned as Lopez and Knowles. They, on the other hand, learned to confine themselves in girdles in order to approximate more closely the flatter proportions of the mainstream standard. Lopez and Knowles are, however, at the light-skinned end of the Black colour spectrum. I firmly believe that their almost-white features allowed their large buttocks to be accepted on the mainstream standard.

It is interesting to note that in the film *Dreamgirls*, Knowles plays the role of a woman whose physical features, body weight, skin colour, and hair are deemed to be more acceptable to white audiences than full-bodied, darker skinned, curly-haired Black women. The film revolves around the fact that she is made the lead singer over a woman who has a more ample body, and who is not as light-skinned and white-looking as Knowles's character. It was an important story to be told, given how historically accurate it is in terms of demonstrating how the standard works.

I am not so naive as to think that society suddenly came to the conclusion that African physical features are okay. About hair, however—Black women's hair—I am suggesting that Black women's natural hair rates low on the mainstream yardstick of beauty. I would even go so far as to suggest that there is a manipulative push against natural hair in mainstream society. This push manipulates many Black women, and Black people in general, to conform to the hegemony in which they live. Thus, many of them push themselves, their daughters, and others around them to live within, accept, and internalize definitions of what is beautiful hair.

...me ah say ah one man...

I sported a low-cut Afro when I returned to live in Antigua in the 80s. I went jogging and swimming twice a day, and it was sheer freedom to be able to submerge myself in the sea without a thought about hair-grooming. Before this, I had taken my low-maintenance hairstyle for granted, but during my four-year so-journ in Antigua, I gained a new appreciation of the ease of having low-cut, natural hair.

One day, while jogging on the beach, I came upon a group of men who were preparing to leave. I noticed that one of them was staring at me, and as I jogged past where he was standing, he said to his friends in a loud voice tinged with mocking cruelty: "Me ah say ah one man!" (I thought it was a man). Then he laughed right in my face. I don't know where my quick response came from, but it was direct and to the point: "Me would say you need glasses!" My response shocked the man into silence, and his friends all laughed. As I jogged away, pleased at how a rejoinder had arrived in me so swiftly, so neatly, and so roundly, I felt as if I had scored one for Afro'd hair women...and as I have done time and time again over the years, I felt despair at the hostility and frontal attacks unleashed on Black women with Afro'd hair, and especially short Afro'd hair. It was bad enough to have journeyed through the media assault on the criteria of beauty but to have it rained down on my head by Black folks was a real travesty.

I started wearing my hair in a low Afro in 1968, and over the years,

I have often experienced insults about looking like a man. The insults did not always come from men; there were women who expressed their dislike of the hairstyle with the same kinds of brazen, in-your-face insults. Sometimes, insults would arrive from women with a veneer of goodwill, as they attempted to impose their disapproval of my natural hair: "You looked so much better when you had your hair straightened." One woman—a *Black* woman—asked me how it was that when my hair was straightened it had been so long, yet now that I had an Afro it was so short. She obviously forgot about the magic of the iron-comb—a tool with which her own hair was well acquainted! What was interesting, too, is that she would repeat the question each time she saw me, even though all I did in response was to smile enigmatically. She was convinced, I believe, that if she said it often enough, I would go back to straightening my hair. Years later, I figured out that her investment in my hair being straightened was caught up in her own image of herself. At the time, I had no such insight; I was walking my way through a new sense of self, and negative comments merely added weight to the journey.

...stories held in the heart...

I had conversations with several Black women about their hair. This was not a formal, or even an informal, study; I was simply curious about whether they had received negative comments about their natural hair. I was struck by the similarity of the experiences of Black women in North America, the Caribbean, and England. A perusal of websites also revealed that negative comments about Black women wearing their hair in its natural state are even more commonplace than the small sample that I had uncovered.

The personal stories are overwhelming in their sheer numbers, and by the similarity in content. One woman reports that some of her family members are unsupportive of her natural hair, and tell her: "You look so nice with long hair" and "Your hair looked so pretty when you had it straightened." In other words, it is not all right to *be in* this world in the way that we *came into* this world. The pressure to conform with straightened hair is back full-force—maybe just as badly, if not worse than it was before the Black Cultural Revolution of the 60s and 70s...before Black people, women in particular, declared by their natural hair to themselves and to the world that Black was beautiful.

I loved my Afro haircut and did not feel that it made me look less feminine. On the contrary, not all men (unlike the man on the beach in Antigua) pretended to or really did mistake me for a man. Often, my low-cut head attracted some men's hands, and I would tell them that I did not appreciate their lovingly caressing my low-cut head, while telling me how sexy it felt. These fondling acts happened in public, as I had no intimate relationship with these men. They were merely acquaintances. I discovered in speaking with other women friends who have had or still have low Afros that the experience was not unique. They too fend off head massages from men with whom they are barely friendly or, at best, have platonic friendships.

The head massages notwithstanding, I wish I could say that I've received as many compliments as I have experienced the insulting call of "man-head" and "bald-head" from both men and women. During the 60s and 70s, the admired Afro was a part of what one "put on" to *be* Black. It was a part of the identification of a person who was Black and proud. Along with this were items such as a Malcolm X or Huey P. Newton poster on your wall, and Coltrane, Miles, Monk, Bird, and Pharoah Sanders records. The Afro was a part of the uniform of Black men and women who wanted to show themselves, each other, and the world how proud they were of being Black. Those were indeed "the old days." And in those "old days," Afro'd heads were given nods of approval by the righteous-thinking members of the *hep* community that young Black people wanted to belong in, and to emulate.

...bliss in a straight-hair world...

With the absence of a mass Black cultural consciousness, more and more Black women are finding their bliss in a straight-hair world. It seems clear that the standard has returned with a vengeance to long, straight hair. Today, the standard includes not only straightened hair but also hairpieces and/or weaves. And it seems that the standard-bearers are not just content to wear and/or admire the standard; sometimes, they invest energy in negating its opposite. There are times when wearing natural hair in today's cultural climate feels like being fully clothed in a nudist colony.

We are aware of course that popular culture reflects the standard determining beauty in hair in every crevice, nook, and cranny of society. Women in the entertainment industry appear on children's television radar really early, and forcefully. And the rigid beauty standard is nowhere more evident than it is in this vehicle that transports and interprets popular culture. Women in the entertainment industry such as Whoopi Goldberg, India.Arie, and Lauryn Hill, who wear their hair in its natural state, stand out. The voice of the standard has gone so far as to take shots at natural hair in situation comedies. An episode of Queen Latifah's show *Living Single* comes to mind. It featured a group of four African American women, one of whom wore her hair in dreadlocks. She was the one character with natural hair. In the episode in question, she was going through a rough emotional experience, and Kim Fields's character, with a toss of her own store-bought, long, straight hair, suggests as a remedy: "Go buy yourself some hair!" Interestingly, in real-life, Kim Fields wears her hair in dreadlocks.

Divorce Court Judge Mablean Ephriam was furious
when the Fox Network replaced her on the popular
television show because she refused to wear a wig
over her own hair. She had taken to wearing the wig
when a salon process made her hair fall out, but
wanted to discard it when her hair recovered. The
network claimed the wig was easier to style.

Judge Ephriam speaking at a press conference in
April 2006:

"The requirement also comes very close to a vio-
lation, if it does not in fact violate, the Fair Employment Practices Act. An employer cannot demand
one to wear a particular hairstyle unless it directly af-
fects or impacts the employee's ability to perform
his or her employment duties. My hairstyle does not
meet this criteria. It is, however, a racial and ethnic
issue.

Suddenly, after seven years of a show that has run
neck and neck with the other top-rated court shows,
why is my hair an issue? Why, I ask? Because of my
ethnicity: African American, Black, Negro, whatever term you prefer to use. Because of my genetics
(short, curly hair), which requires the use of chemicals and/or a hot pressing comb to straighten and
curlers to style. It cannot be styled by a wash, blow
dry, and set. Therefore, in Fox's opinion, it is a
time-consuming issue.

I wore a short hairstyle, which was my own hair.
Due to a misapplication of a chemical process, I lost

a substantial amount of hair in season six. Out of my desire to maintain continuity, and the image I had created (for the last five years), I elected to wear a wig last year. Had Fox asked me to maintain a short hairstyle for continuity and for image, it would have been a different issue. But they are saying I must continue to wear the wig because that would expedite the hair styling process. However, my hair has now grown. I had not yet decided what hairstyle I would wear for season eight. If I were to accept their demands, I would have been unable to make that decision.

...Barbara Walters and black women's hair...

Even the usually professional journalist Barbara Walters has jumped into the fray about Black women's hair. Recently, on *The View*, Walters carried out what can only be described as attacks on three Black women. In one instance, it was a verbal attack surrounding body hair, and in the other two other cases, using her hands, she actually physically pulled the hair on their heads.

The first incident is shameful: she took the curiosity about Black women's hair to an all-time low by asking actor/comedian Monique if she shaves the hair on her legs and under her armpits. Monique, who is an outspoken woman, stood up and showed off the hair on her legs. Then she explained, as if speaking to a child, that the hair under people's armpits can stink, and thus, would, of course, need to be shaved.

In another segment of *The View*, Barbara Walters asked actor and singer Brandy: "Is that your real hair?" And before Brandy could respond, she put her hands on Brandy's hair and pulled it. When it did not budge, Walters was undaunted; she asked again, still tugging at Brandy's hair: "Is this your real hair?" A shocked Brandy finally found her voice and retorted: "Well, it ain't a wig!"

The third incident occurred with Tanika Ray, a TV host. Walters caressed Ray's hair, then pulled and tugged it, just as she had done with Brandy. Ray's reaction was swift; she moved her head out of reach, saying: "She's pulling it!" Then she said in a firm voice: "It's not coming off, Barbara." When Walters finally backed off, Ray explained that her hair is "wash and go." She ends: "I'm a lucky girl." Walters looked as if she wanted to put her hands in Ray's hair again but Ray turned to face her, moving her head out of reach; and so the incident ended. I have no doubt that Black women are going to soon write into their contract with *The View*: "My hair is not to be touched and/or pulled by Barbara Walters, or any other hosts of *The View*."

Dread and the Baldhead

*All the days of the vow of his separation there shall
no razor come upon his head: until the days be
fulfilled, in which he separateth himself unto
the LORD, he shall be holy, and shall let the locks
of the hair of his head grow.* Numbers 6:5

I have spent what is tantamount to a significant number of years of my life in hair salons and/or barbershops having my Afro trimmed. Along with what I consider wasted time is the fact that it costs a pretty penny to keep the trimming going, so I hit upon a plan: grow dreadlocks! But...the joke is that dreadlocks take more grooming, and it costs more in the hair salon to care for locks than it does to have a haircut! So I grew locks to avoid hair salons but I'm back in them because dreadlocks require much more grooming than a low Afro! Isn't that a howl?

I arrived at the conclusion that locks were easy to take care of, mistakenly believing that all I needed to do was stop combing and/or cutting my hair. So I simply sallied forth into letting my hair grow. The result was a rather scrappy-looking head of hair that resembled dreadlocks but was really not even dreadlocks's distant cousin. The journey to that realization took time and much vacillation, resulting in my eventual capitulation to the professional fingers of a hairdresser.

I did not decide on my own to go to a hairdresser: a friend took pity on me. One day, sitting behind me in my office, she got a good view of the mess at the back of my head, and said gently, smiling, and touching my arm: "May I introduce you to my hairdresser? Her name is Carlene, and here is her phone number." I laughed uproariously at her honesty, and thanked her for the referral. And so it was that a week later, I was sitting in a hairdresser's chair having my dreadlocks receive much needed attention. With deft and gentle fingers, my friend's hairdresser, Carlene, twisted and pruned my unruly hair, and quick as a flash, my dreadlocks emerged and stayed put. After that, I visited her salon every couple of weeks to keep my hair looking groomed. Any diversion from that schedule, and the unkempt, fuzzy-haired look would return—just the way it was before my friend introduced me to Carlene.

So there I was, back in the place from which I had been trying to escape: a hair salon every couple of weeks to attend to my head. Carlene took pity on me and showed me how to take care of my dreadlocks between visits to her, and so now I only visit her when I need a major "tune-up." Things have settled into a nice, manageable pattern.

...Althea Prince is in the house...

Fast forward to two years after this move to dreadlocks. I was at a function where it was announced from the podium: "Althea Prince is in the house!" At the time, I was out of the room, and returned to find out that someone, after hearing my name announced, had been looking for me as he had grown up around two of my nephews and my younger brother, all of whom have had dreadlocks for many years, by the way.

I found out later that this friend of my nephews and my brother had approached someone who had dreadlocks and asked him if he knew Althea Prince. He told this person that his reason for approaching him was, he said, he knew "the Prince head" (that is, dreadlocks) and figured that this person with dreadlocks would know who I was. And indeed, the person he approached is a good friend of mine. It is ironic, however, that during the many years of our friendship, I sported a low Afro. So dreadlocks cannot be seen as a link between us. Interestingly, if the friend of my nephews and my brother had looked for me with dreadlocks more than two years ago, he would have been surprised to find me a "bald-head" or a "man-head."

...women with man-head...

That incident brought up a memory of an in-law who was quoted as having described the women in my family to the maître d' at a hotel as "...a group of women with man-head." I wondered what that relative would say if he could have heard that a few years later, another person expected to find me with dreadlocks and had not been disappointed. I consider it odd to see it as a mark of identification of a family when you have only known three members of a very large family with similar hairstyles. It is, after all, just hair— the stuff that grows on top of our heads. It is, in my view, malleable...I can do what I want with it. One thing I do know, and have known from the first time I experienced it: I do not enjoy straightening my hair...the hot iron-comb passing through it from the time I was about age fifteen always left an alien scent that I was never able to tolerate. I continued straightening my hair with a hot iron-comb, as did all of my friends, but I secretly hated the process. I have an acute sense of smell, and so I used to walk around all day, conscious of the alien smell of my hair...it had been fried with a hot comb, and I could still smell it. I remained conscious of the smell until I washed my hair, every couple of weeks, but of course, I immediately ironed it again. My straightened bangs also made my forehead greasy and shiny...and eventually, I would get pimples underneath my bangs.

As did all women who ironed their hair, I used to get burned from the process, which resulted in sores on my head. When they formed scabs, they too carried a smell that I could not tolerate. Sometimes, I would burn my ear, or the back of my neck, and then I had a visible sore for as long as a week or two.

When Black women started cream-straightening or perming their hair, I resisted...it was not that I didn't want my hair cream-straightened but I heard many stories of hair and scalps being burned by chemicals. In addition, given my many allergies, I could not tolerate the toxic fumes that rose from your head when the process was taking place. I had been in hair salons when it was being done to other women, and always had to leave the room. I realized that there would never be a day when I would be able to go through that process...so hot iron-comb it was...and the sores in my head continued to plague me...and the smell from the process continued to make me sick to my stomach...and I continued to get pimples on my shiny, greasy forehead.

Of course, it never occurred to me to stop straightening my hair; that was a given. I simply learned to live with the discomfort. I wanted to look pretty, and the terms for that included straight hair; I never felt that I had any choice. In fact, it just did not come up. None of my friends discussed why we straightened our hair; it was just something we did as soon as we were old enough to obtain permission to do so. By the time we were fifteen, most of us had begun the hot iron-comb-on-the-weekend ritual.

Stokely Carmichael and Miriam Makeba

"If imperialism touches one grain of hair on his head, we shall not let the fact pass without retaliation." Fidel Castro, in reference to the alleged U.S.A. plot to assassinate Stokely Carmichael

It was political awareness—not my pimply, shiny, greasy forehead, or the sores on my head—that sent me under the shower to wash out my straightened hair and "go natural." One day (circa 1968), I heard Stokely Carmichael—a radical voice of the 60s—speak eloquently of the beauty of Black people, and the power of the call: "Black is Beautiful!" At his side sat his then wife, Miriam Makeba[1], natural and beautiful in every way. She was regal in a flowing, African dress, and I just knew from looking at her that she would never allow herself to do what I was doing to my hair. She confirmed this in her speech about her journey as a South African woman who was living in exile because of her public statements against apartheid. She was indeed a clear-thinking woman...I knew, instinctively, that she would never allow herself to experience a hot iron-comb, nor would she tolerate the sores that were, at that very moment, carrying out a riotous itching in the crown of my head. There was beauty in Miriam Makeba, just as she was; there was beauty in me, just as I was.

I wondered: for what, pray tell, was I enduring the torture of ironing my hair, and sometimes even paying for it to be done to me? I never had a problem with my natural hair; I just followed the going trend that dictated that beautiful hair was straight hair. I thought natural hair was okay. I thought straight hair was okay too, but my hair was not straight; and the process I had to go through to make it straight was painful, costly, and gave me pimples. I did not know it but I needed an epiphany, and I got one!

...from epiphany to action...

Stokely Carmichael and Miriam Makeba's speeches did the trick in helping me to reassess how I wore my hair and why I straightened it in the face of such discomfort. After listening to them, I went home and put my iron-comb-straight-head under a cascading shower of water, and I have never looked back since. I had had my epiphany!

I understood that there was something strong and powerful about being comfortable with what one embodies, including the stuff that grows on top of one's head—it too was a part of my body. I could not internalize the words "Black is Beautiful" while I felt that my hair in its natural state did not meet the beauty mark.

It was an exhilarating moment. For the first time in my life, I felt free of the burden of my hair. The burden was far heavier than if I had been aware that I was carrying it; once lifted, its weight was immediately recognizable. Besides the practical nature of the freedoms that natural hair brought, there was the bonus of being able to look after my own hair. I returned to the rows of Congo that I had learned to plait as a child. The Congo plaits brought reproachful stares from Black women but I persevered. Then, in 1979, a white actor, Bo Derek, appeared in the movie *Ten* wearing cornrows, and the whole world went wild on braids after that.

I also wore my hair in an Afro, bringing even more stares—this time from both Black and white people. Again, I persevered. Many people had Afros but we were only around each other at Black community functions. In the rest of our lives, we were outnumbered—usually the only Black person in school, or on the job—stared at, and interrogated: How does it stand out like that? Do you wash it? Those kinds of questions were from white people; from Black people there were no questions, there was criticism.

What was I building on? My mother had never straightened her hair, and it looked pretty good to me. She never dyed it either, and would coif her thick, grey hair just with her fingers and a comb. And my father? I remembered that on more than one occasion, he had suggested that I cut my hair like Odetta, the singer...she wore her hair in a low Afro for years before it became popular. He was onto something because Odetta looked fabulous. At the time, however, wearing my hair in its natural state was out of the question as everyone else had straightened hair! As a child, my hair had been something that seemed too coarse and tough for the adults in my life to manage. Coupled with all of that, when I was a teenager, the icons in popular culture all had straightened hair, and so did the beauty queens who entered the Carnival Queen competitions in Antigua. The winner was always someone light-skinned, with straight or straightened hair.

After I started wearing my hair in its natural state, I returned to Antigua for a visit, and I can still remember the delight in my father's eyes when he saw my Afro. He reminded me that he had always suggested that that hairstyle would suit my face. Until that moment, I had quite forgotten how much he used to object to his daughters' straightening their hair. My mother gave in to our desire to go with the flow, but my father had always thought that we were much more beautiful with natural hair. Clearly, he was rather before his time in many ways, as he always had great appreciation for what he called "pure Africans." His skin colour, for example, was always a thing of pride for him; he was jet-Black, so Black that the palms of his hands and the soles of his feet stood out starkly against his blue-Black skin.

In my hair journey from childhood to my epiphany in 1968, I came to recognize that as a Black woman, my experience had specificity to it. It contained a detail that is common to all Black girls: natural, curly hair is not considered beautiful and needs to be straightened. Black girls meet this horrible judgement as soon as they begin their pubescent walk to and through adolescence. And as they grow, they face this denial of the self over and over again. They come upon this hurdle at a time when their appearance matters so much to them that they are willing to withstand anything to be more beautiful. They are willing to endure pimples on their foreheads, burn sores in their heads, the smell of permed hair, and the hole in their pockets, or their parents' pockets, for the cost of keeping the "do" in place.

Black girls' and women's choices concerning their hair are dictated by external standards of beauty that they have internalized. This beauty standard has to be accepted within oneself before it can be seen to be a real, free choice that one makes to straighten one's hair with the creams that have now replaced the hot iron-comb.

I know that it is difficult to go against the grain. I am, however, concerned when judgements about a natural part of a young

Black woman's body is dismissed by the beauty yardstick. This is especially worrying when these judgements come from the commercial marketplace, and/or from popular culture, and from young men who are influenced by them. These judgements about what is beautiful have a large impact on young Black women's self-esteem, their choices, and, ultimately, their lives.

The media has focused as much, if not more, attention on the hairstyle of Rep. Cynthia McKinney, an eleven-year veteran congresswoman as it has on her grassroots political style. In one article in *The Washington Post*, McKinney's two very different hairstyles are the focus. Reporter Robin Givhan scathingly dismisses her earlier hairstyle: "Who could notice the cheekbones, the nose, and the smile with the loaded distractions of that washerwoman crown of braids?" Finally, the journalist described her hair which, as a Black woman, I think looks like a twist-out as "... standing all over her head."

McKinney's new hairstyle then comes under fire: "Her hair, which she had for years worn in thick braids, seemed to be in a limbo between a polished Afro and a head of funky twists. Had the humidity gotten to it?"

Meanwhile, Neal Boortz, [who is white] speaking on his nationally syndicated radio program, said that Rep. McKinney's new hairstyle made her look like "a ghetto slut," "an explosion at a Brillo pad factory" and "Tina Turner peeing in an electric fence."

On his own website, Boortz went even further, describing McKinney's hair as making her look like "ghetto trash." Finally, he pleaded, "Get a braider over there...quick! Nobody with a modicum of self-respect would go around looking like that. And don't give me any stuff for saying this. I've endured years of 'bald' remarks. I'm entitled."

Rep. McKinney had been involved in an incident

with a police officer at a Capitol Hill security check-point and allegedly struck the officer. Boortz did not state it directly, but he is clearly implying that because of her hairstyle, the police would have justifiably mistaken Congresswoman McKinney for "ghetto trash," a "ghetto slut," and thus prevented her from entering Capitol Hill. Although, why should anyone's hair, per se, disqualify them from going somewhere?

NOTES

1. Miriam Makeba is a singer from South Africa. Stokely Carmichael was a leader of SNCC—Student Non-violent Coordinating Committee, and Honorary President of The Black Panther Party. He was later invited to live in Guinea-Conakry by the President, Ahmed Sékou Touré, and exiled Ghanaian President, Kwame Nkrumah. In their honour, he took the new name Kwame Touré

Michelle Obama, the First Lady of the United States of America

...musings on the media, sister-black women, and Michelle Obama's hair...plus, Chris Rock discovers his daughter wants "good hair"...

Chris Rock has stated publicly that Black women's hair costs more than anything they wear. He was describing women who are perhaps overly preoccupied with their hair—so much so, that they regularly spend long hours in hair salons, straightening their hair and/or adding extensions and weaves to it.

Any Black woman can look at Michelle Obama's hair and tell that she spends a minimum amount of time and money on her hair. There are no visible extensions, although some people do suggest that there were likely, from time to time, a few add-ons for a fuller look. All in all, however, the First Lady demonstrates a laid-back attitude to her hair, sometimes simply pulling it all back into a bun. I notice that she wears her hair straightened, dating all the way back to when she was a young lawyer.

What, I wonder, is Michelle Obama saying to her two young daughters about why she straightens her hair? Do they ask to have "good hair," as Chris Rock reports that his daughter did? Rock says that when one of his daughters asked the question, "Daddy, why don't I have good hair?" he realized that there was a problem about which he knew little. His daughter's question prompted him to make the documentary film *Good Hair*, looking at the subject of Black people's hair.

When I heard Chris Rock speaking about how his daughter's question rattled him, I thought again of the Pecola character in the Toni Morrison novel *The Bluest Eye*. Pecola yearned for blue eyes in order to be beautiful. Clearly, Chris Rock's daughter was expressing a similar kind of yearning for feeling right about herself. She had come to feel that her hair was not "good hair," not hair that others in her world considered "good."

As Barack Obama drew closer and closer to winning the Democratic nomination for president, I noticed that Black women began to focus on Michelle Obama's hair. They talked about her clothes as well, but not with the same attention and passion with which they focused on her hair. Indeed, the "sisters" were having their say on what some simply referred to as "the hair." The daily comments raged on, full and furious, as the inauguration drew closer and closer. Finally, the big day arrived, and most agreed that she'd done the sisters proud with her demure pageboy, and with her roots nicely cleaned-up (straightened). She had allowed some natural roots to show on occasion, and that did not go down well with the sisters.

Patricia Williams[1] in *The Daily Beast* commented: "While curly hair, twists, short Afros, and cornrows are all much more prevalent and tolerated these days, those choices are still publicly interrogated to an unseemly degree." She went on to note that the

New Yorker cartoon that satirized Michelle Obama as an armed revolutionary made a point of depicting her with Afro'd hair. Williams suggests that that hairstyle is considered "political hair." She describes it thus: "We're talking unequivocally, implacably, no bones about it, political hair."

I would go one step further to suggest that if Michelle Obama had had a natural hairstyle, it might have been a political problem. The problem would have crossed racial lines, twinning African Americans and other Americans in a chorus about her radical hair, or again to quote Williams, "...the universalized angry Black scalp." As we have seen in the cases discussed in earlier in this book, Americans generally seem to speak with one media voice when it comes to Black women's natural hair. "Redstar" on the *Blacksnob* blog said of Michelle and the issue of "political hair": "She's got incredible style, but I think she needs a softer hair look for political purposes."

Elizabeth Wellington, fashion columnist for *The Philadelphia Inquirer* suggests that what Black women across the country wanted to know was: "Who did her hair? Was she fresh from the chair? What kind of relaxer does she use? Did Oprah lend her Andre?" She was ultimately declared "a no-lye lady"—that is, no chemicals were used; it had been blown-out. Michelle Obama had accomplished, the article went on to say: "Hair nirvana—without chemicals." And of course it was bound to happen: the manufacturer of a product used on her hair claim on their website that one can "Get Michelle Obama's Look" with it. Her hairdresser must suffer questions about his client's hair that he discreetly ignores: Is she natural or does she relax? Does she colour? Is that really her hair? The interviewer reports on the questions, and I now report on there being no answer to the questions; and yet, they persist... and they will, for this is an all-important part of a Black woman's persona.

All in all, Black women have declared that Michelle Obama's hair is politically correct. According to some Black women, as the president's wife, she cannot afford to have "political hair." In other words, her hair cannot—no pun intended—make waves...it cannot be seen as offensive.

Some Black women with whom I have spoken in Toronto, and in the U.S.A., said, with serious certainty, that for the First Lady, natural hair would be too Black, too "out there," too strong. This is the thinking, despite Michelle Obama's Harvard degree, and vice-presidential, corporate job status in health care. So now we have it clearly on the table that there are some Black people in the U.S.A., Canada, and likely in other parts of the world who declare that the hair with which they were born is unacceptable. What is a person to do when the hair with which she was born is considered offensive and is held in a place of disrespect? Well, it depends on what she wants to accomplish, my respondents assert.

I see their point very well. Michelle Obama has declared her intention to be successful in the role she has taken on. Clearly, making strong political statements with her hair would not be her most politically astute action. She likely figured this out during her tenure in the health care industry and certainly would have known it as a lawyer. She strikes me as a person who has a good understanding of the society in which she lives. As First Lady, she has much more at stake than she did in any of her earlier occupations. Indeed, this would not be a good time to make waves. Given the kinds of bashing that Black women have taken in the media about their natural hair, Michelle Obama would be considered a strange lady if she suddenly went from straightened hair to natural hair. That would be a major political minus for her husband, and would likely cause ripples with more than just Black people. The cartoon on the *New Yorker* cover made this patently clear. And now, she sails on as First Lady with hair that is clearly politically neutral.

It should be noted that other Black women in politics and the communications media have worn their hair in natural styles, although in Canada and the U.K., this has been less of an issue. Canadian Liberal MP Marlene Jennings wears her hair in a natural "do," and in Britain, Labour MP Dawn Butler wears her hair in dreadlocks.

I know of no other racial or ethnic group for whom hair is such an issue that it becomes the focus of so many people's comments—regardless of the political work in which they are engaged. For Congresswoman Cynthia McKinney, the focus almost derailed her career. And so long as braids, dreadlocks, and Afros continue to be considered socially radical hairstyles, Black women in public life will always have to include their choice of hairstyle as a factor in developing their profile.

Indeed, I believe there is no other group of people for whom their natural hair is a problem in the public sphere. The hegemonic import of this is mind-blowing! What then is a body to do? What does Michelle Obama choose to do? So far, she appears to be doing just what suits her.

As First Lady, Michelle Obama draws comments on just about every little thing that she does or does not do—it goes with the territory. Lately, the focus has shifted from her hair to her bare arms. They have graced everything from *Vogue* magazine to her official White House portrait. As negative and positive responses fly across the media, one notable pundit, Jack Cafferty, declared that her arms are becoming "the stuff of legend." He confesses that he is developing a crush on Michelle Obama, and says of her effect on the White House: "It's like the sun came out and a fresh spring breeze began wafting through the open windows." He asks: "Who appears sleeveless on the cover of *Vogue*, let alone in front of a joint session of Congress while her husband delivers one of the most important speeches of his life?" Finally, he admits that when it comes to the First Lady, he is smitten!

In 2008, The New Yorker magazine in the U.S.A. carried a cover with a cartoon depicting Michelle Obama with a large Afro, a gun on her shoulder, fist-bumping Barack Obama, dressed in Muslim clothes. In full view an American flag burns in the fireplace.

NOTES

1. *The Daily Beast*. January 28, 2009. "The Politics of Michelle Obama's Hair." http://www.thedailybeast.com/blogs-and-stories/2008-10-09/the-politics-of-michelle-obamas-hair

To Locks or Not to Locks

...email correspondence with my niece Janis...

Janis to Althea

I can't wait for tomorrow evening so you can go get your locks!

Althea to Janis

I got me locks! BTW, is who tell those Af/Ams that the word is spelt 'locs'? I saw lotsa hair books with locks spelled locs...them have nerve! Anyway, I got me my young dreads. They are soooo lovely...I keep on looking at me'self in the mirror since I got home...and grinning. They look amaaaaaaazing! and then some... forward orrrn Janis...can't wait to see them on you...wow! The hairstylist agreed with me that that would be Mansa's best 'do'... So maybe she will arrive at it like we have...suddenly, in her later years (well, you are not at all "later" years, but later than you had first thought of them)...for me it's both kinds of "later" years. Yes indeed, I got young dreads! This is the most exciting thing that has happened in my young life for the year...I've got to get out more!

Tomorrow I am attending an open house, and I am now divining the outfit to go with my young dreads. I even got out some flashy silver earrings and a kinda matching silver Navajo bracelet that I bought in Las Vegas...you know, silver, laced with ancient blackened workings. Yes I! Bring orn de bredren-dem!

Love,

Moi!

Althea to Janis

I am so excited me'self! My hair is now wa-ay longer than I've seen it for years! And it is as thick as it used to be when I was very young...I forgot that that's what happened to it as it grew. I remember that Jennifer [niece] and I had the same kind of hair: thick, coarse, and heavy...So I suspect my locks will be pretty similar. She has her locks dyed a reddy-bronze; I don't know if you recall. I was thinking of going to gold ma'self. Seriously; cuz the grey is something I dye; I figured I could just as easily go to gold locks...that yaller-gold locks configuration. But I'll let them be quite a bit longer before going to gold...kind of gold/bronze. We'll see. I am quite excited. I have wanted locks for about twenty years!

Wow! I cannot imagine what took me so long, but like you, it was looking at the hair and thinking, "What do I do next?" I had to do something and I was really tired of doing twists once a week.

I think seeing Gabrielle [niece in the U.K.] do nice styles, also Gerald [nephew in the U.K.]...he's quite adept at moving it into different ways...ties it up, using some locks for the tie, etc. Gabrielle does some stunning do's...so do my friends in Toronto... So locks it is!

I am sure that there are good locks folks somewhere in Tampa; but with Mechelle's [stepdaughter] help you could do it yourself, of course. Your hands may get tired for the work at the back, but that's where Mechelle could help. Let me know how you get on.

Althea to Janis

Subject: URGENT

Forgot to tell you that the hairdresser warns against wax. As the hair grows, it cuts into the hair, and eventually, the individual locks are weakened and break within the locks. So the locks that start out with wax eventually need repair from the process...it takes a while to happen. The hairdresser used hemp, which can be obtained from health food stores. He also suggested glycerine, or just a leave-on conditioner for the dampness to do the twisting.

Note after the fact: I have found a really good hair-caretaker of natural hair... Flamboyant Hair Salon...owned by a wonder-worker named Carlene.

Janis to Althea

Well, I haven't done mine yet. Been wearing a 'twist-out' these last two weeks. Know what that is? Two strands twists and then wearing them undone with a headband to keep the hair back. I looook very young with that "do."

Last week I met a woman who has Sister Locks—I think that's the spelling. That's some process by which the lock is done on some machine or some something like that. Very nice looking but expensive! Has to be done by someone "licensed." See how folk find ways to make money? I do like the way they look, but not keen on spending that kinda money.

I also got the number of a Jamaican woman who does a friend's twists...That I do myself but I called her to see if she will do some cornrow for me...Then asked about locks! She has locks herself, and does them. Very reasonable prices she quoted. So I'mma go tomorrow for the cornrow and see her locks. She says she uses *cassie**—strained...and doan know what's needed to "lock" quicker. Then uses a gel with a tiny bit of beeswax (she mentioned the breaking and collecting of dirt with the beeswax). You know anything 'bout using *cassie* for this?

last words from Althea
In the end, I maintained my locks and Janis did twists on occasion, finally re-straightening her hair...mildly...with a flat iron (see "Who I Am is In My Hair" by Dr. Janis Prince Inniss). It is very attractive. There are numerous new ways to make Black women's hair a glorious celebration at the top of the head.

*acacia—called "cassie" in the Caribbean

look what the future hath wrought

by Mansa Trotman

Chemically treat it
straighten it
perm it
texturize it
relax it (gently of course)
more like fry it
is it burning?

Don't scratch
Try to ignore the smell
Highlight it
Rinse it
Dye it
Permanently colour it
spiral curl it

'til it grows out
dry it with a hand-held spray of hot air
moisturize it
cover it with a plastic cap
pull it back
tease it
frizz it
mousse it
gel it
hairspray it
make sure it has extra hold
holds like glue
so the curls won't droop
the style won't fade
headband it so the roots won't show

or if it's been more than two months
you're best to cover it
or use the old trick
of handfuls of Vaseline and blow-dryer
damage
breakage
split ends
conditioning treatments
olive oil and mayonnaise
placenta
super-grow formula
natural herbs and
steam treatments
because we can't deviate from the norm
gotta have long, straight hair

for him to run his hands through and not get stuck
it's gotta have bounce
it's gotta have body
can't look like a duplicate of him
gotta look like a woman with
hair that swings when you walk
hair that moves when you laugh
hair that he can run his hands through and not get stuck
so what will us women do next?
in our bid to maintain the norm, we really did deviate
because the norm before us, before our mothers,
actually it was
before their mothers
was kinky hair
thick hair
hair that didn't have to swing
hair that didn't have to move
hair that didn't have to have a hand to go through it, unstuck
to validate its worth.

Related Books and Films

Books

Hair Matters: Beauty, Power and Black Women's Consciousness by Ingrid Banks. New York University Press. N.Y. 2000.

Nappy Journey: The Twisted Road to Natural Hair by Sharon D. Chappelle. Authorhouse. 2003

Good Hair: For Colored Girls Who've Considered Weaves When the Chemicals Became Too Ruff. By Lonnice Brittenum Bonner. Three Rivers Press. 1994.

Hair Story: Untangling the Roots of Black Hair in America by Ayana Byrd and Lori Tharps. St. Martin's Press. 2001

Being Black by Althea Prince. Insomniac Press. Toronto. 2001

Films

Black, Bold and Beautiful: Black Women's Hair
Directed by Nadine Valcin. Produced by Jennifer Kawaja and Julia Sereny. Sienna Films. Canada, 1999, 40 minutes, color, VHS [documentary]

The Body Beautiful
A film by Ngozi Onwurah. British Film Institute. England, 1991, 23 minutes, Color, VHS/16mm/DVD [documentary]

Perfect Image?
A film by Maureen Blackwood. Sankofa Film and Video Collective. England. 1988, 30 minutes, Color, VHS [documentary]